D0016895

Finishing Touches for Teens

**Beauty, Etiquette, and Self-Esteem
For Your Changing World**

Linda G. Wilder Dyer
Author of *Pretty Me: A Handbook For Being Your Best*

Illustrations by Sherri Faye Caldow

J
646.704
DYER
c.1

Clairebrooke Press

Copyright © 1991 by Linda Wilder Dyer

All rights reserved, including the right to reproduce this work in any form whatsoever without permission in writing from the publisher, except for brief passages in connection with a review.

For information, write:

Clairebrooke Press, a division of,
Pretty Me, Incorporated
2129 General Booth Blvd.
Box 300
Virginia Beach, VA 23454

Use of this work as course or seminar text is prohibited without the expressed written consent of the author. Courses and seminars are available for girls ages 6 to 11 and 12 to 17 based on *Pretty Me: A Handbook For Being Your Best*, and *Finishing Touches For Teens*.

Please address ordering inquiries to:

Hampton Roads Publishing Company
891 Norfolk Square
Norfolk, Virginia 23502
(804)459-2453
FAX: (804)455-8907

Cover design by Patrick Smith
Illustrations by Sherri Faye Caldow

ISBN 1-878901-12-5

Printed in the United States of America

For Ashley and Elizabeth - my precious daughters
and my husband, Courtney.

Many thanks to the Leggett Stores
who believed in our company.

Thank you to our wonderful instructors
and to P.J. Forbes

Table of Contents

Introduction

Inside Out, Head to Toe,
Get Excited — Here We Go!

Hi there! Welcome to 14 chapters of a book that's fun to read and will probably change your life forever. If you're interested—read on!

Just how do I know it will change your life? Well, first, being a "tween" (ages 11 and 12) and a "teen" (13-17) are the stages in your life when the most drastic changes occur. You started out loving dolls and ended up loving the boy on your bus. You woke up this morning and your bangs didn't do right. You're mad at your Dad. You weren't in the mood to clean up your room, or hang up your clothes, you're a super loyal friend and a great girl. Am I close? Read on.

You'd change your hair (nothing drastic of course!), sell your kid brother to the Gypsies, shrink your thighs and burn your clothes in a heartbeat.

By the time you get home from school you've changed your mind on all of the above. Your parents want 10 teenagers *just* like you. Your hair has never looked better, and you even read "Marvin" his bed-time story.

Confused? Of course not! You're a girl, and you're changing every day.

I wrote this book for many reasons, but the main reason is to help you always feel good about things you do and say, and about the way you look and act. No matter where you go or who you are with, I want you to be at ease. I will help you know what to do and what to say to make growing up a little easier. Your teen years should be exciting and happy times, times full of questions and answers, discovery and exploring.

It is my sincere wish that growing up be the happiest of times for you.

Linda Wilder Dyer
Virginia Beach, VA 1991

II.
The Best Inner Me Make-over

Chapter 1
Being your Own Best Friend

If you have it, you don't need to have anything else; and if you don't have it, it doesn't much matter what else you have.
Maggie, in Sir James Barrie's Play,
What Every Woman Knows

What is the character Maggie speaking of? Charm. Charm is a rather nebulous term. It means many different things. It can be visualizing yourself as a success, being the best you can be and also realistically setting lifetime goals. A "charming" person just seems to have it all together—almost all the time. But—that's not *really* all there is. There's a lot more to "being your own best friend."

In all of the hundreds of classes that I've taught and thousands of girls I have taught and advised over the past twenty years (ooh—20, that's a scary thought!) the most effective tool I've found to help all of us reach our potential is "visualization."

Visualization is the process of actually "seeing" and imagining something and feeling what it would be like as a reality. I want you to learn how to visualize yourself as the successful, happy person you aspire to become. Use your imagination!

Your teen and early adult years are such an exciting time—a time of discovery, self-reliance, apprehension and curiosity (to name a few!).

You're going to need a healthy dose of self-confidence to help guide you through some of the turbulence ahead.

So—let's start working on your own personal "personality puzzle." I know you've put a puzzle together before. Do you have small children in your home? You've probably noticed how small puzzle pieces seem to get lost pretty easily. My six year old gets frustrated when she's putting a puzzle together and happens to be missing just one or two pieces. But I try to help her realize that she can still tell what the picture will be, even if she's missing a piece or two. Developing our own puzzle is a lot like that. You may feel confident about your overall appearance or secure with your personality but still feel that you need to fine tune a few "missing pieces"—perhaps public speaking, developing a special talent or finding that perfect hairstyle that really works for you.

Some of your missing puzzle pieces may be:
* The way you talk
* The way you walk—your body language
* Your study habits
* Your figure
* Your hairstyle
* Your personality
* The way you think of others
* Your fashion personality
* Learning not to procrastinate
* Your health and nutritional needs

You can probably think of others that apply specifically to you.

Look Inside Yourself
Take an honest look at yourself. It's one of the first things any of us have to do before we can change anything we don't like.

What I Like About Myself	**What I'd Like to Change or Improve**
_____	_____
_____	_____
_____	_____

I'm sure you hesitated filling the first column. My students throughout the years *always* have. Remember, there is a difference between self-confidence and conceit. Feeling good about yourself is a very special part of your "Jigsaw Puzzle." So is being honest enough with ourselves to admit that work needs to be done in some areas and that we all have limitations as to what we may be able to change.

A fifteen-year-old girl in one of my lectures a few years ago asked if I thought she could be a model one day. She was less than 5'2", had dirty hair with no style, bright red chipped fingernail polish and heavy, heavy makeup.

When I explained to her that it was difficult to break into modeling when you're under 5'6" she balked and said that she was just as pretty as any girl she'd ever seen in a teen magazine. True—she was pretty, but when I asked her how she felt about changing her hairstyle and make-up technique, she told me that, quite frankly, she liked them just the way they were.

Her unwillingness to change the things she *could* change made it difficult for me to advise or encourage her further towards her goal of becoming a model.

Change is healthy, but we are all "creatures of habit" and it's hard to visualize ourselves differently once we've become comfortable with a particular look or attitude. Learn to trust the opinion of others whom you respect and look up to.

Your ability to think positively and objectively about yourself comes with gaining more self-confidence.

Self-confidence is the way you perceive and judge yourself. It is influenced by your successes, your failures (I hope they are few), your experiences in life and the many people you'll encounter.

Let's take a look at how a person with self-confidence differs from a person without self-confidence.

With

Loves a new challenge
Takes responsibility for successes as well as failures
Can make own decisions
Assumes that success is the end result of their hard work

Without

Afraid to try new things
Fear of failure
Need lots of reassurance
Assumes that people will be displeased with their actions

You do not have to be a certain age, height, weight,

nationality or "look" to be popular and confident. What comes to your mind when I say the word confidence. Is it the secret sense of knowing what to do and when? Do you know girls who always seem to do the right thing at the right time while you shuffle around awkwardly? The answer is probably yes; not necessarily because you *are* awkward but because you may lack the confidence and positive self-image it takes to be confident.

Go easy on yourself. Growing up doesn't happen all at once. Maturity and a sense of "self" take many years to nurture.

If there was a magic pill you could take to make you the most popular, confident girl in your school, would you take it? Your answer is probably a very emphatic "*yes.*" I am certain that many girls have wished for such a pill since time began. Popularity seems to be the main goal for girls; more important sometimes than good grades. Being in the "right crowd" at school certainly can seem like the ultimate goal. But will it really assure you of happiness and success?

Not everyone can be a cheerleader or the Class President. Find the special things that you do best and enjoy the most. Become a master of those things and do not dwell on the things that are not your specialty. Concentrate on being the very best "YOU" that you can be!

If it makes you feel any better, even the "popular" girls have moments of insecurity. Absolutely *everyone* has felt as though they could crawl in a hole and die, at some time.

What do you notice about the people who seem to possess popularity and a sense of ease? Let's discuss a few. Add a few of your own if you think of others.

Sense of Humor: My personal favorite, and without a doubt this is the one trait that has helped me out of potentially embarrassing situations. Appreciate others and look for things to laugh about—especially yourself! Learn to laugh *with* people, not at them.

Good Relationships: Having a mutual respect for your parents, siblings, step-brothers, step-sisters and step-parents. Always allow them the same courtesy that you expect.

Appreciate Beautiful Things: There is beauty all around you...learn to notice it frequently. It can very simple...a flower, the coo of a new baby, a special friend, freshly mowed grass. Nature gives us so many wonderful things to cherish. Don't waste all of this beauty! It's yours for the taking.

Healthy Emotions: To express sincere, spontaneous surprise, joy, happiness, even sorrow, should come naturally. When an emotion is too "staged" or "dramatic," it will be obvious.

Be an Interesting Friend: Although it's always easier to talk about things that are familiar to you, you must also practice the ability to listen and learn about those around you. You may be pleasantly surprised at the wonderful knowledge you may gain from others.

Caring and Graciousness: Be kind to others in your heart. Refrain from gossip and jokes at the expense of others. Try not to be stingy with praise and compliments.

Self-Confidence: Believe in yourself. Do daily mental exercises to boost your self-esteem. We all need an occasional boost to the spirit. If you truly practice that, "If you can believe it, you can achieve it," you will not be disappointed!

While we are on the subject of popularity and getting along with others, I would like to share some valuable information with you. First of all, I have always been a big sister to my many students over the years. Although I am a mother myself, I tend to hear a lot of things from my students that perhaps they would not feel comfortable telling most adults. If you are ever asked to do something that you do not believe in or agree with just for the sake of being popular, please stop; think; and remember that following your head as well as following your heart are usually excellent guidelines. As you become an adult, you will never regret your good judgment.

At times you may feel that having good manners, obeying rules and being a charming young lady are not

7

"cool." There is no easy way to prove these things to each of you. It takes a great deal of trust. Hopefully, it is the trust in your family and especially the trust in yourself, that will ease the transition of growing into a lovely adult, inside *and* out.

Feeling Comfortable "Making" Conversation

Conversation is defined very simply as, "the act of more than one person discussing a single topic or more than one topic with another."

The last time you called one of your friends and talked about what a surprise the English test was today, you had a conversation. A conversation is normally based on a pleasant subject. Sometimes, grown-ups just call it "chit-chat." It is light and easy, usually.

An argument, on the other hand, is also a conversation, only not very pleasant. It is a conversation between two people on a subject with which they disagree.

A conversation is certainly more pleasant than an argument, but none of us is going to go through life without a few conflicts or disagreements. Loud talking and fussing is not conversation. When you are upset about something, you should wait until you are alone with the person or persons who made you feel that way. Having someone confront you in the hall at school when all your friends are there is very embarrassing and will, most likely, cause even more hostility. Anger is what turns conversation into confrontation. Usually, people who are insecure become boisterous around others. Perhaps they are in need of attention. Have you ever noticed that sometimes the students in school who most often get in trouble and act up in class are the same ones who are really shy and in need of a true friend deep down inside?

Occasionally, someone will try to get the upper hand or act tough, or maybe even get on the defensive when you approach them only because they do not have the self-confidence that it would take to explain their point calmly.

One of the easiest math exercises you will ever learn is that "Two wrongs never make a right!" Be as calm as you can be whenever you are explaining your opinions. You do not ever want to be accused of being difficult or hard to get along with.

Now, don't misunderstand; it is perfectly acceptable to disagree with someone if you are certain that you can do it without being bossy. No one likes a "Miss Know-it-All." There is nothing wrong with expressing your own ideas or standing up for what you think is right.

The tone of your voice has a lot to do with how your friends, family and acquaintances will react to what you say. If you try to make a point or state your ideas about something in a loud voice, everyone might think that you are ready to argue. If you are in a group and everyone is trying to make a point at the same time, it is really tempting to talk louder so that everyone can hear what you have to say. Resist the urge to do that. Sit back patiently and wait your turn to talk. When you do talk, use a soft, but confident voice. You know what I do when I'm in a group and everyone is trying to talk at once? I walk away and lose interest in what they *ALL* have to say!

We've discussed a little of what conversation is, but now let's discuss some of what it shouldn't be.

Too Personal

Stay away from questions like "How much money do your parents make?"; "Why don't you live in a bigger house?"; and, "Why does your Dad drive that old car?" Think about how embarrassed you would be if someone asked you that kind of question! Now, I didn't say that questions were taboo. Quite the contrary. Questions are probably the very best way to get a conversation going; it is the *type* of question that you ask that makes the difference.

Instead, try something like, "You must be new in the neighborhood. Where did you live before?" Or, certainly one of the easiest ones for you would be "What school do you go to?" or "Did you take a vacation this summer?"

Just remember to always try to put yourself in the place of the person being asked the question. If it is something that you would

not feel comfortable asking, then they probably won't either.

Unpleasant Subjects

It's one thing to talk about a biology experiment if you are with a group of your friends in the same project. But I wouldn't recommend it if you are having dinner with your friends parents. Generally, dinnertime is not a great time to discuss such subjects as parts of the body and how they work, the horribly gross accident you heard about on the way home, or someone's very sad news. Subjects such as upcoming school projects, new friends you made, church activities, or hobbies are much more acceptable. The same rule applies here that applies in almost all other cases—if it's a subject that you would not want to hear about, maybe others wouldn't either.

Too Fast or Too Slow

Trying to pay attention to someone who is talking "a mile a minute" is not only annoying, but frustrating. A person who talks too fast sounds nervous; when a person sounds nervous when they speak, we sometimes tend to question the value of what they have to say. You may find yourself chattering away if you are very excited. If you just made the cheering squad, or made the chorus, you have every right to be excited; just remember to take your time and speak clearly.

Being around someone who speaks too slowly is just as annoying. Have you ever sat patiently while a friend dragged on and on with a somewhat boring conversation? You wouldn't want to hurt your friend's feelings for the world, but you begin to wonder how much longer you can sit and be attentive. What do you do? You may do one of two things; first, you can sit quietly and be as patient as possible, or if you have a great deal of self-confidence and timing, you can slip in a question about the subject to show your friend that you are not only paying attention but you can hardly wait until they finish their exciting story!

Me, Me, Me!

Speaking of boring subjects. Girls who only know how to talk about their own accomplishments tend to get boring and annoying very quickly. They take over a conversation telling about all of the wonderful things they have done. I have found from experience that if someone is really that great, you will more than likely hear about it from another source.

Being proud of something you have done is perfectly all right; in fact, it's great! Just resist the temptation to talk only of what you have done and leave out the other friends included. It's alright to say "My parents just bought me a horse! Do you enjoy riding Jessica?" This way you'll bring your friends into the conversation instead of leaving them on the sidelines listening to how wonderful *you* are!

You will receive many more compliments if you follow those rules. A compliment is a pleasant gift. It makes you feel proud inside for knowing your hard work paid off— somebody noticed! Give compliments freely. It doesn't cost a penny and you will make someone feel so special.

Introvert or Extrovert?

Which one are you? You're probably asking what in the world they mean. Let's take the word "introvert" first. The prefix of this word is intro; the first syllable is "in." A person who is an introvert stays into himself. They do not tend to speak up very much. Sometimes, introverts are very shy. However, sometimes an introvert is just very cautious about what they say and how they say it. When they speak, you usually listen. Their words are weighed very carefully.

An extrovert, on the other hand, is just the opposite. They are bubbly, outgoing and tend to turn strangers into acquaintances with ease.

Is there a right or wrong way to be? Not really, as both traits have their good points and bad. An introvert may miss out on making new friends, voicing an opinion or being included in social activities. An extrovert might be so busy talking they may forget to be a good listener. What is right is what's right for you. If you are perfectly content being an extrovert, and you will allow yourself the ability to include and listen to your friends and you do not come on too strong, then enjoy your gregarious personality.

If an introvert is secretly wishing she could walk to the other side of the room and introduce herself to new friends but cannot because of the butterflies in her tummy, she needs to practice some conversation and confidence-building skills. (Always taking a friend with you helps, too.)

Friendship

Friendship makes life more fulfilling—more exciting and fun! Your ability to make new friends will depend on how much self-confidence you have and whether or not you're an introvert or an extrovert.

What do you look for in a new friend? What attracts you to the people you like and associate with? Do they:
* like the same clothes as you
* have the same interests as you
* go to your school
* go to your church
* have cute big brothers
* have the same hobby as you
* have the same goals as you
* practice the same morals as you

Whatever the similarity, it certainly is easier to be friends with a person you have something in common with as opposed to someone without any common interests.

Think about the people you are friends with. Why are they your friends? Friendships should be mutually beneficial. You wouldn't want to hang around with a girl who only likes you because your cute big brother sang in a popular band and she thought she might have an "in" because of you. You can't begrudge her reason, but there needs to be another reason for pursuing the relationship with you. Benefits of a friendship should be balanced between the two individuals involved. When the balance is constantly one-sided the friendship may be in danger of falling apart. Or, it may simply be a matter of a friendship rut or lack of communication.

Friends don't gossip about one another or constantly criticize. You should be able to make suggestions to a friend in a caring manner without making the person feel inadequate.

You'll have occasional disagreements and misunderstandings with friends—that's perfectly normal. You may even get on each other's nerves from time to time, but clear up any misunderstandings before they get blown out of proportion.

Getting Mixed Up with the "Wrong" Crowd

Sometimes we want so badly to be accepted or to look grown-up or "cool" that we allow ourselves to associate or hang around with a group of people who may not be good for us. When you're with the "wrong" crowd you may not feel like you're really being yourself. If they smoke or drink or talk nasty you may feel pressured to do so for the sake of fitting in.

You may not really be having fun at all, but you want so badly to be accepted that you compromise your ethics or rules for living. Be true to yourself. If something feels like it may be wrong, it probably is wrong—and certainly not right for the kind of happy, successful person you're becoming.

"Boy People" and Dating

The decision to date and when to start dating is one that you'll make with your parents or guardian. Initially, you may feel like that's the hard decision, but before long there may be even harder decisions before you. Who will you date? Will you date only one boy? Are you afraid of rejection? What will you say to him? Do you feel any pressures?

Ask your parents how they met. What was their first date like? Where did they go? Did they feel nervous? You'll be surprised at the similarities between dating then and dating now. Sure, the music, the clothes and perhaps even the type of place they went was different from what you'll do now, but boy-girl relationships haven't differed too much since time began!

The first similarity is that boys and girls start out in elementary school acting like they can't stand one another. Have you ever heard the story about the little boy who had to start wearing eyeglasses in the third grade? His mother feared that he would be embarrassed and upset at this new addition. However, he came home the first day and cheerfully explained that he loved the glasses. "The bullies don't hit me and the girls don't kiss me!"

The first time I really remember being interested in a boy was fifth grade. I wanted to impress him. I wanted to be perfect. I wanted to be funny and witty and cute!

What I ended up doing was devastating.

My girlfriends and I always tried to sit across from "him" (I'll call "him" "Clifford") and his friends. Everyone was eating and telling jokes. I was just taking a huge swallow of my orange drink when "Clifford" delivered a particularly funny punchline. In a split second he was drenched in the orange drink that I spewed across the table as a result of my hysterical laughter.

I could have died. I never really knew if it made the difference, but "Clifford" married a skinny cheerleader after graduation from college.

My social savvy around the opposite sex eventually improved and today I am happily married and have two terrific daughters. But, that wasn't without a few "toads" thrown in for good measure.

The only way you will meet and eventually find "Mr. Right" as an adult is to date different boys and not "put all off your eggs in one basket" when you're young.

Some boys will end up being better "buddies" than romantic interests. You'll meet many different boys with many different interests. Boys like for you to discuss *their* interests. If you have a date with someone who loves golf and you don't know a birdie from a bogey, I'd suggest you pick the brain of an avid golfer before your date. It'll make you feel more comfortable and your date will feel special too.

Review the tips for making conversation in this chapter.

But, don't worry needlessly about exactly what you'll say and how you'll say it. If the two of you really like each other it will just "click" and it will feel right and comfortable.

Bad Reasons for Dating a Particular Person

* You can gain status because he's the captain of the football team.

* His sister is in a club you'd like to join.

* His father owns a business you'd like to work for.

* He has a neat car and you'd feel really cool riding around town in it.

* He lives in the "right" neighborhood and you've always wanted to meet other people your age who live there.

* He's really good-looking and the two of you will look great walking together.

Boys don't like to be manipulated or used any more than anyone else. Don't act interested in someone if you're really not and don't be ashamed or embarrassed to date someone who may not be exactly what your image of Mr. Perfect was. You may be very pleasantly surprised.

In closing, learn to love others as you learn to love yourself. Don't be afraid to talk to the lonely girl in Biology. Perhaps she's just shy. Don't be timid about approaching your parents about a personal conflict. Chances are they'll understand. Building confidence in your many relationships builds the "network" that forms a happy, meaningful life.

Chapter 2
Thoroughly Modern Manners

Having a secure knowledge of the basics plus the self-confidence it takes to adapt traditional values to the many situations you will encounter as you meet new challenges is the goal for this chapter.

We'll discuss:

* Etiquette of writing letters, notes, and invitations
* Telephone Etiquette
* Dining Etiquette at home or a restaurant
* Etiquette is defined as the group of rules of social conduct that dictate what our society deems proper and acceptable behavior. We are able to conduct ourselves more effectively and mannerly when we understand what is expected of us.

While I certainly believe that learning the fundamentals of etiquette provides an important knowledge base for you, I also firmly believe that you must use common sense. Knowing the basics enables you to follow the rules to a "T" or deviate from them when necessary and appropriate.

The Write Stuff

It seems that the Female has always been the "social director" of the family. In years past women seemed to have ample time to keep up with written correspondence, as well as other types of mannerly obligations.

It was her responsibility to make sure that birthday, anniversary and new baby greetings were carried out. She was also expected to handle the necessary responses to wedding announcements, funerals (ordering floral tributes, memorials and assisting with household obligations), as well as Bar/Bat Mitzvah, luncheons, teas, dinner parties and more! Is it any wonder that ladies in years past had their hands full with family and social obligations? Having an additional career or working outside the home can make it difficult to keep up with other details such as remembering to send Aunt Lucy a birthday card.

Girls, please keep a calendar! I can tell you from experience (and embarrassment) that it's crucial. When I got married my husband needed (expected?!) me to keep up with his family's birthday's, anniversaries and other special occasions. One of the first things I did was copy all of the names and dates into my calendar book. At the beginning of each new year I transfer all of the information into a new calendar book.

This calendar, datebook, or appointment book will start to feel like an extra appendage before long. I consult my appointment book each day, but especially on Sunday in order to prepare myself for the week ahead. Please don't keep more than one calendar at a time. It's too easy to neglect making double entries. However, one helpful idea is to keep one family wall calendar (I keep mine in the kitchen) for *everyone's* obligations; Dad works late, Ashley has choir, Elizabeth to the Doctor, etc.

Your Paper "Wardrobe"

I'm convinced that half the battle in getting written correspondence out on time is having the proper supplies on hand, rather than running to the store every time you need a birthday card or a thank you note. A thank you note, for example, should be handwritten on a note card. Some ladies like to use a printed note card with "Thank You" printed on the front. I prefer to purchase plain fold-over note cards in white, ecru, or soft pastels so that I can use them for other types of notes. That way, if someone surprises me with a lovely gift or gesture, I can sit down immediately and acknowledge it!

Any stationery you choose makes a statement about you—just as your wardrobe does. Your name or monogram may appear on your stationery. The nicest paper to use is 100 percent cotton fiber. White or ecru with black print is the most traditional and is always appropriate.

Monogrammed notes and letter sheets are elegant, classy and timeless. It's rather comical to know that something so classy has such lowly roots. In medieval times illiterate members of royalty used their monograms or initials to authorize documents and proclamations!

The components of your stationery collection may eventually include:

Fold-over notes (monogrammed or plain)

Informals—small white or ecru fold-over notes engraved in black with a lady's complete social name preceded by her title (Ms., Miss, or Mrs.).

Message cards—These single cards are large enough to mail in a small note-sized envelope. They are usually white or ecru and engraved in black. The lady's full social name, preceded by her title appears centered near the top of the card with her address printed in the upper right-hand corner. They are used for greetings, replies to formal invitations, and for hand-writing informal invitations.

Correspondence Cards—Slightly more informal than a note card, these note-sized one-side cards are printed on heavy paper and may be in a pastel or have a bordered edge. The lady's name (without title) or monogram may appear centered at the top of the card. You may use these for short, informal notes or thank you notes. Please only write on the front.

Postcards—When engraved, it is done with one line at the top of the postcard. The usual size is 4" x 6." The correspondence should be simple, and obviously non-confidential.

Half-sheets—A piece of formal stationery that fits into it's envelope folded in half is called a half-sheet. They may be embellished with name, address, monogram or name and address combination. You would never write on the back, so order plain second sheets if you tend to be long-winded! Your envelopes will match in color and style. Here again, they are normally white or ecru and can be used as you would a note card.

Letter sheets—These are the most formal papers in a lady's stationery collection. They are ecru or white and engraved in black with a fold along the left-hand side like a formal wedding invitation. It is folded in half from top to bottom to fit in an envelope that is half it's size. A letter sheet would be monogrammed or embossed with the lady's initials. They can be used for any kind of correspondence.

Stationery—The most basic paper you'll own. It does not have to be engraved and can be a color, if you wish. Envelopes should match. As with any other proper paper, use only the front. It will be folded either in half or in thirds to fit into the envelope.

There will be many occasions in your life when you will need to write a note or a letter. How many can you name?

* Thank You Notes
* Business Letters
* Notes of Condolence
* Invitations
* Friendly Letters
* Memorandums

Most of the personal correspondence that you do now will be handwritten. A lady's handwriting says a lot about her. It can very well be an indication of how careful and cautious, how well-groomed and neat, how meticulous and even how organized she is. Wow! I'll bet you never thought of all that when you did your homework last night!

With just a very few exceptions, all of the people that I know who have sloppy handwriting also need to practice their neatness in other ways.

Thank You Notes—I hope you'll need to write many of these in your life! Writing a thank you note is appropriate whenever you receive a gift or a nice gesture from someone. Birthdays, graduations, weddings—any special occasion when someone would receive a gift—even Christmas and Chanukah would be a lovely idea.

Don't forget to write a nice note if you have been someone's house guest. What a special gift that is! If you have been an overnight guest for a weekend or more, a small hostess gift is appropriate; perhaps potpourri, gourmet preserves, or maybe some guest soaps.

Letters—Communicating with people on paper is to

21

write a letter. It costs less than long distance phone calls and can be fun and creative as well. Write a letter very naturally, just the way you would talk. A reminder—the back page of a letter sheet is never written on.

There are a few simple rules to remember when writing"

1. *Date*—Goes in the upper corner of your paper.

2. Salutation—The greeting line of your letter is placed above the body of the letter; Dear Josey, Dear Mr. Anderson.

3. *Body*—This is your opportunity to "speak" in your letter. Use proper grammar and keep your dictionary and thesaurus close by. If your letter is neatly done and well planned, the person receiving it will think highly of you. Get in the habit of writing nice, neat, interesting letters, even if they are only for chit-chat among friends. As you grow older, the letter writing skills you will have acquired will benefit you greatly.

4. *The Closing*—Is normally "Love," or "Affectionately," if it is a close friend or family member, but "Your's truly," or "Sincerely," would be appropriate for a more formal acquaintance.

5. *The Envelope*—Make sure your envelope is addressed properly. Don't start the address up so high that there won't be room for the postage stamp, and please don't forget your complete return address just in case anything goes wrong and your letter needs to be returned to you. Listing your name in the return address is optional.

Keeping a Journal

Have you ever kept a diary? Recording your thoughts and personal feelings on paper is both therapeutic and quite special.

I recently ran across a diary I started when I was in the third grade. It was so funny to see what I had listed as my favorite song, dance, book, activities, and who my closest friends were. I'll share this with my daughters one day and I'm sure they'll think it's hysterical.

A girl your age in the late 1800s would have probably kept a journal. In fact, she may very well have faithfully written in her journal each and every day of her life.

Those pretty fabric covered books with blank pages that are available in gift and stationery shops make lovely journals. I received one as a gift that was a combination journal/appointment book.

Each evening after everyone's asleep I pull out my journal and my favorite fountain pen. I can "un-load" all of my joys, frustrations, brilliant ideas that I'm sure will change the world, and anything else noteworthy that happens to be on my mind. There's something about having that time to myself to write before going to bed that is pure bliss!

Treat yourself to a beautiful journal and a special pen— perhaps a fountain pen.

Writing in your journal will also serve as a great way to practice beautiful penmanship.

If you ever have the opportunity to examine the hand-writing skills evident in the Victorian era (the period beginning in 1837 when Victoria became Queen of England and continuing through the 1890s) you'll notice that it resembles calligraphy. You may enjoy taking a calligraphy class so that you can adorn your journal with lovely writing. You'll have something very special to pass down to your own children one day.

Telephone Etiquette

There is no doubt that the telephone will be a constant companion to you throughout your life. As a student, its use will enable you to catch up on homework; as an employee, it may be crucial to your daily responsibilities; as a parent, it may help you arrange a surprise birthday party for your daughter!

As a teenager growing up, it may seem like a physical addition to your body!

Have you ever had an adult ask you if the phone was permanently attached to your face? Depending on how many people share the telephone in your home, your parents may set down some livable guidelines.

If your parents conduct business from home, your telephone time may be limited. Some families have separate telephone lines for the kids or teens in the household. Most people, however, do not enjoy such a luxury.

Your personal phone calls may be limited to five or ten minutes and may also be limited to certain times during the day or evening. Please adhere to the rules for telephone use in your home.

A very important part of telephone etiquette is knowing when to place a call and when not to place a call. The "nine-to-nine" rule is a good general one to follow.

Calls placed prior to 9:00 a.m. on weekday mornings can interrupt an already hectic time of getting ready for school and work. I had a friend in high school who phoned me almost every morning around 7:00 a.m. to ask me what I was wearing that day! It drove me nuts (especially when she showed up looking like my twin sister).

After 9:00 p.m. is usually a time when families are trying to "wind down" from a hectic day. Most children and teens are in bed if its a school night. I try to avoid placing phone calls after that hour if possible.

I realize that it may sometimes be necessary to place calls either very early or very late, but try not to make it a habit.

Let's review a few reminders:

* Dialing a wrong number by mistake is normal and everyone does it occasionally. Hanging up without acknowledging your error is rude. No one will begrudge you if you simply state, "I'm sorry, I've dialed the wrong number."

* Have a pad and pencil available for messages next to each telephone. When taking a message, indicate the time of the call, verify the spelling of the caller's name if you're in doubt, and always repeat the phone number back to the caller for verification.

 * Always identify yourself when placing a call, even if the person answering the phone is a friend. Also remember to identify yourself if your friends' parents answer the phone. You may see Kelli's mom every day, but she may not automatically recognize your voice.

 * The typical rule of who ends the phone conversation is based on who placed the call initially.

 * Always ask the person you've called if it's an acceptable time to talk. "Hi, Katie! Got a minute to gab?"

 * Never *insist* upon the identity of a caller if the call is for another family member. Wrong: "Who's calling?" (too abrupt); Right: "She's not available right now. May I have her return your call?"

 * Please don't hang up when someone's answering machine answers their phone. Leave *some* kind of message; even if its just the time and your name and number. I realize that not everyone feels comfortable talking into a machine, but it is extremely frustrating to receive mystery hang-ups on your recorder.

 * Is the tone of your voice pleasant? Record your voice and play it back. You may be surprised by what you (or others) hear. Are you monotone, too fast, too soft, or too "mumble-jumble"?

 * Each family will have their own acceptable way to answer the phone. Do the adults in your home want their last name used? "Hello, Vance residence." "Good morning," "Good afternoon," or "Good evening" may be a pleasant deviation from just "Hello."

 * When you answer the phone and it's for someone else, say "Just a minute, please." Put the phone down *gently* and go find the person. Please don't stand there holding the receiver and scream "MOM, IT'S FOR YOU!"

 * When you're placing a call to someone and they're not home, don't just say "Okay" and hang up. Say you'll call the person back. (You may want to ask when they're expected home), or ask if you may leave a message for the friend to call you.

 * Always say "Good-bye" before hanging up.

Dining Etiquette

When you're just a small child, you have a good excuse for not having proper table skills. But now you are a teenager and a teenager will be going to lovely restaurants, dining with friends, adults, and *boyfriends*. Imagine how embarrassed you'd be if your peas slid off your fork or your sliced tomato shot across the table! These horrible things will probably never happen to you, but let's just make sure that you're prepared to handle whatever situation comes your way.

Some of you may be lucky enough to enjoy meals at the dinner table as a family each day—but maybe not. In fact, in most of my classes, the students indicate that at least half of them don't have that opportunity as much as they would like. Why? Different people with different schedules, coming and going, rushing around grabbing a cookie here, a snack there, a fast food burger in between. What it all boils down to is that not all kids get a chance to form good table manner skills at an early age. It doesn't mean that their parents don't care or that they don't care—it simply means that we live in times where life can be hectic. For example, your mom may get off work at 5:00 p.m., your brother might need to be at soccer practice at 5:45 p.m. and you might have a dance class at 6:15 p.m. Meanwhile, dad picked up your sister from the sitter and they're both at home starving! Realistically, I can tell you what happens in a lot of families—Dad feeds "Sis" and himself, Mom arrives home an hour later after you and your brother have convinced your mom to pull into the neighborhood "drive-through." Sound familiar to anyone? Unfortunately, it probably does. I won't go into the nutritional side of this right now (we have a whole chapter for that). The main thing that may be missing is the routine that is necessary to form good table manners at home.

Where the "Tools" Go

What tools? Some call it silverware, some call it flat-ware, others may call them utensils. Whatever they are called, they are used to get your food from place to place while you're enjoying a meal. Once you become familiar with each piece and what it's used for, the fear and mystique of table etiquette will vanish forever!

The Difference Between Flatware and Holloware

Flatware refers to all knives, forks and spoons, including those used in serving foods.

Holloware refers to all dishes, bowls, tea sets, trays, salt shakers, candlesticks, pitchers, and other pieces used for table service or decoration.

When you hear the word "sterling," it means that there is a very high standard of purity in the silver. Under United States law, only pieces that contain the proper amount of pure silver can be stamped "Sterling."

Place Setting Pieces

Although most ladies like for their "silver" to match and be of only one "pattern" or design, it is perfectly acceptable to mix pieces if they are family heirlooms. In fact, it can be a very charming effect. Please do not put silver in the dishwasher as it would be much too hot and abrasive. Wash it gently by hand in warm, soapy water. Dry it immediately and put it back in a silver drawer or chest.

Basic Table Settings

Most ladies use what is called a five-piece place setting. This includes a place knife, place fork, place spoon, salad fork and teaspoon.

Eventually, ladies like to add serving pieces to their

collection such as a gravy ladle, pie server, vegetable serving spoon or a cold meat fork to name a few.

Relax....Enjoy!

There are many correct ways to set a table. In most cases, all you have to do is just think about what you are eating and place the utensils in the order they will be used. The outside pieces are used first, then work in towards your plate. When in doubt, follow the host or hostess and do it the same way they do. That way, if they are wrong, at least everyone will be wrong the same way!

There are two ways to eat with a knife and fork: the European method and the American method. The European method is much easier. Leave your fork in your left hand after cutting your food and feed yourself with your left hand (easy for us lefties!). The American method uses sort of a "cross-over" motion. Cut your food with your right hand. Put your knife down, switch the fork from your left hand to your right hand. Finally, you get to eat!

Although there is no right or wrong way, you may find after practice that the European method is a little easier.

When you are finished, your knife and fork will go side by side on the top right side of the plate and cross the plate diagonally. The tines (or prongs) of your fork should face down, and your knife blade should extend about a 1/2-inch over the side of the plate.

Using this *finished* position is a lot nicer than pushing yourself away from the table and moaning, "I'm stuffed!"

However, if you just need a minute to let your food settle or to contemplate another buttered roll, use the *rest* position which is simply forming an "X" in the center of your plate by crossing the downward tines of your fork over the blade of your knife. Again, clear about a 1/2 inch over the edge of your plate.

My advice to you is that as long as you don't make your mistake obvious and draw great attention to it, it will probably go unnoticed. There's no reason to be so nervous and self-conscious of whether or not you're using the right fork at the exact right moment that you won't enjoy the fine food and pleasant company.

Obviously, you are not going to use every utensil and dish each time you dine. In fact, there are several pieces that you probably won't use for a few years, such as the wine glass and the cup and saucer. A full, formal table setting is for special occasions, holiday meals, or surprising your parents on a special day.

Additionally, courses may even be added to this table setting such as an **appetizer**. In this case, let's say it's a seafood cocktail.

The seafood cocktail is eaten with the pronged fork on your far right. It is called a seafood fork. When you are finished, place the fork on your plate. Do not eat the leftover cocktail sauce; in fact, don't do *anything* with the leftover sauce.

If **soup** is being served, it comes before the salad, and the bowl will be placed on top of your dinner plate. The soup spoon will be larger than a teaspoon. Always dip your soup spoon away from you and sip from the edge of the spoon without slurping. Do not be tempted to lift the bowl to get the last drop! Leave your spoon on the side of your dinner plate when finished.

The Salad Course

Your mother may serve **salad** in a bowl at home because it's easier to eat, but actually, a salad should be served on a salad plate. In nicer restaurants, your salad will be brought to you on a chilled plate immediately after you have finished your soup course (provided you had one). The waiter or waitress will simply switch your soup bowl and soiled spoon for your fresh salad. Look up at your server at this point and say "Thank you." It is important to be courteous to the people who serve us and help us in public.

A salad should be in pieces that can be easily eaten with your salad fork and not need to be cut. That doesn't always happen though. I'm the first one to admit that if a slice of tomato would look prettier left uncut on my finished salad, I may be tempted to leave it that way for serving purposes. It is, therefore, acceptable to cut your salad as you enjoy it. Salads are truly one of my favorites. Not only do they look pretty, they're so nutritious.

The Bread & Butter Plate

The small plate in the general area above your forks is for bread, crackers, and butter. There may or may not be a small butter knife placed horizontally across the top portion of the plate. Take bread or rolls as they are passed around the dinner table *one at a time* only, even though you are positive you could eat two. After you finish the first one, decide if you have room! Break off small bite-size pieces and butter them only *as you are ready to eat them.* This procedure is done directly over your bread and butter plate. The butter knife stays on the top portion of the plate when not in use. Oh, please remember, don't put a *mountain* of butter on your plate. If the butter is wrapped in foil, place the folded trash on the bread and butter plate.

The Entrée

The **entrée** is the main course, such as beef, poultry, fish, pork or pasta. It will usually be served on the same plate with a choice of potato, rice, pasta, and a vegetable. You may choose to enjoy your entrée with any remaining salad.

The Dessert Course

I have always remembered how to spell **dessert** by knowing that since lots of people would like to eat *doubles* that there are double S's in the word! (It may sound silly, but it works.) Most desserts are very easy to eat because they only require a spoon or fork. Some types of desserts may require that you use both, such as cakes with gooey or runny fillings. Use common sense and do what will be less messy. If the fillings or sauces contain fruits that are too large to be eaten whole, it's alright to cut them first.

The Fingerbowl

Although they are not used very frequently, a finger-bowl serves an important purpose when present. Strong smelly seafood dishes or fruit desserts that may stain your fingers or table linens and other stains can be easily removed with a fingerbowl of cool water with a slice of lemon floating in it. The lemon removes odors, and when rubbed on the skin, can sometimes take away stains.

Setting the Mood

I am a true believer in setting the proper atmosphere in which to eat when setting the table. Many times when I have prepared a relatively simple meal, I am praised because the table looks so nice. Having an attractive table helps to make the most ordinary meal special. Be creative. Bring some fresh flowers in from the garden, try a nifty napkin fold, or plan a "theme" table such as Tropical Beach Party, an indoor picnic, or a Victorian Tea. Use your imagination.

"Dining With a Date" Restaurant Reminders

* When choosing a selection from the menu, choose neither the least expensive entrée nor the most costly. You don't want to insult your date, but you also don't want to devastate his budget.
* When a headwaiter, host or hostess is present to seat people, ladies follow directly behind him or her with gentlemen bringing up the rear. If no restaurant person-nel in such a capacity are present, the lady follows the gentleman as he finds a table.
* It is proper for a lady to advise her date (or any

gentleman she is dining with) of their menu selection. She will speak directly to the waiter regarding choice of vegetable, salad dressing, etc.

* Don't let your "eyes be bigger than your stomach." It would be embarrassing and unfair to your date to waste food and money.

* If you happen to see friends dining in the same restaurant, it's alright to speak and visit for just a minute, but it wouldn't be right to monopolize their time or to neglect your date. Introduce him to your friends and return to your table.

* If you're eating in a restaurant with a buffet table, don't be tempted to pile one of everything onto your plate at once. Take a realistic amount initially and leave open the option of "seconds." Leave your used dishes and flatware in place and a busboy will remove them while you're at the buffet table. Obtain clean dishes at the buffet line.

* A gentleman stands when a lady approaches the table (not the waitress, though). Likewise, if you should need to "powder your nose," your date should stand and assist you out of your chair.

* A lady doesn't smear lipstick onto a cloth napkin.

Dictionary of Possible Dining Disasters

It's wise to occasionally prepare for disasters—just in case they occur. (You do know, of course, that if you prepare for them, they will never materialize.) Let's discuss some in alphabetical order:

Allergies—Your hostess has just served strawberries and cream for dessert, and they make you break out in 3/4-inch hives. Don't embarrass your hostess by shrieking at the very sight of the dish, nor do you want to bore everyone with a lengthy talk about your allergies and other health problems. Simply say, "No thank you. I don't care for any."

Apples—Apples are not difficult to eat if you're at a picnic. Just pick up a juicy, shiny one and enjoy. However, if you're at the table, please cut in quarters and eat with a knife and fork.

Artichokes—An exciting and nutritious finger food. The leaves are pulled off one at a time. Hold leaf by pointed end and dip lighter colored "meaty" end into the sauce if there is one provided. (It will probably be a lemony, butter and egg sauce called "hollandaise.") With or without sauce, pull the leaf through your front teeth to remove the soft "meaty" part. Keep the used leaves neatly on your plate as you finish. The "treasure" is the cone-shaped heart of the artichoke that you will find after finishing all the leaves. You'll come to a fuzzy part called the "choke." Do not eat this part, but cut and eat the heart. It's a delicacy! (Hint: Have mother buy an artichoke for you to "practice" on at home first.)

Asparagus—If it's cooked, there's no question that you must eat this vegetable with your fork. If it's fresh or lightly steamed, you may eat it with your fingers if it is being served as an appetizer or hors d'oeuvres. The closer to the tip, the more tender and easier to eat the parts will be. Use a cocktail plate or napkin as a helper.

Avocados—When they are served cut in half with the dark, bumpy skin still attached, scoop out and eat with a spoon. If the hollow in the center is filled with salad, eat with your fork. Avocados are very good snacks.

Baked Potatoes—Remove and discard foil wrapping, if present, by rolling into a small ball and placing under edge of bread plate. Season your potato, and eat it with your fork. Cut the skin with your knife and fork. It's full of vitamins and minerals and is a special treat not to be neglected.

Bananas—One of nature's easier foods; it even comes with its own hand-protecting wrapper. However, bananas are only eaten "monkey-style" in a casual setting. If you're ever served one at the dinner table, peel it all the way on a plate, put the skin on the side and cut into bite-size pieces. Ever notice how we all tend to put too much banana in our mouths and end up looking like chipmunks! Well, no more.

Berries—Eat with your spoon as opposed to chasing the rolly-polly's around your plate or bowl with a fork. If you are served whole, fresh strawberries with a dip, pick the berry up by the stem, dip it lightly and bite, taking care not to drip juice on you or on the table linen.

Blowing Your Nose—It's disgusting just thinking about it, but sometimes it just can't be helped. It should, however, be avoided at the table. Excuse yourself to the ladies room. (See sneezing.)

Bread and Rolls—Break off small bite-size portions individually, buttering them as you eat them. Remember, never spread butter on it like you were icing a cake. *Always* do this over a plate.

Burping—Another necessary bodily function that should never be performed deliberately. If it happens, keep your mouth closed (muffles the sound), and say "Excuse me." Absolutely never laugh or giggle if someone at the table burps on purpose. You will only add "fuel to the fire" and encourage that poor soul to do something even worse. In some countries, burping after a meal is considered a compliment to the cook. If you're reading this book, you probably don't live in one of those countries.

Cake—If it is a dry, firm cake such as pound cake that doesn't have frosting or filling, it's alright to hold it on a napkin and break off bite-size pieces with your fingers. Otherwise, use a fork. I've been to several wedding receptions where cake with lots of frosting flowers was served on napkins without forks. Resist the temptation to take the piece with the most icing as you are in for a messy challenge.

Candy— "Oh brother!" you're probably thinking; "*a rule for eating candy!*" This applies to the fancy type that comes nestled in its own little paper nest (mmm—like truffles!). You are to take the first and only one you touch when the box or plate is passed to you. Pick it up, paper and all, and eat with fingers. (Can you resist the urge to pinch out pieces to see what the filling is?)

Chicken—This doesn't have anything to do with the

apprehension you might feel for all of these new table manners to learn! Actually, this delicious, all-American treat should be eaten with the help of a knife and fork unless it is crisply fried and eaten at a picnic.

Choking—Certainly no laughing matter. The international sign for choking is to grasp your neck and reach out for help with the other. I would imagine this action would be automatic if you were really choking. A person in trouble would not be able to cough or talk. Immediately, someone should be summoned who knows the Heimlich Maneuver.

Clams—If you live by the seashore and have an opportunity to try clams or other shellfish, you're in for a treat. When clams are steamed, the shell will open up part of the way, and you can use your fingers or your fork to carefully open it enough to reach in with your fork and lift out the clam. Either dip it in melted butter or cocktail sauce or enjoy the delicious taste alone (all done over a plate, of course).

Corn-on-the-Cob—Butter and season lightly so as not to create a drippy mess. Grasp each securely, either with your fingers or by using the stick-in type holders if they are provided. Do not chomp noisily like a piglet on a farm or chew back and forth like a typewriter carriage!

Dip—In the event that raw vegetables are served with dip, please place a spoonful of dip on your plate along with the vegetables. Do not hang over the "veggie" tray and crunch cauliflower! The same applies to chips, etc.

Fish Bones—"Tiny Terrors!" Beware, as they can sneak up on you quickly. Carefully remove with your fingers and place on edge of your plate.

Fly in Soup, etc.—It rarely happens, but it is a possibility. If it occurs in a restaurant, quietly get your waiter's attention. Do not jump up and down screaming, "Bug! Bug! Help!" That's really not fair. I'm sure you will cheerfully be presented with a replacement and many apologies. If you're a dinner guest in a home and discover an unwelcome guest, don't do *anything* except move to the next course. If a fly drops by and decides to take a dip in your lemonade, that's a different story—ask for another.

Fruit Cocktail—Use a spoon; don't stab the pieces of fruit individually.

Grapefruit Half—There are special grapefruit spoons with a peaked tip that will easily dislodge a grapefruit section from its rind, but if one is not available, use a dessert spoon, being careful to not squirt juice when you dig in. After eating the fruit, you may use your spoon to drink any leftover juice as you would soup. *Please* do not pick up the rind and squeeze it into your spoon, not even in private as you may forget and do it in front of the cutest boy in school someday!

Grapes—The seedless ones are easy. Break a small section of stems off of the whole bunch. *Eat them one at a time*, putting the whole grape in your mouth. If you're eating the seeded variety, take the seeds out of your mouth by removing them into a paper napkin after you have chewed and swallowed the fruit.

Gravy—Use the gravy ladle or spoon to apply gravy to food; don't pour it on like a pitcher. Less is better; more is messy.

Gristle—This is the chewy, fatty substance often found in meats. If gristle finds it way into your mouth, carefully and discreetly expel it into your napkin (paper, if possible) and put it under the rim of your plate. Do not attempt to swallow it. The waiter can bring you another napkin if you are at a restaurant.

Lobster—A real food challenge, but well worth it. If you can master the art of lobster eating, please put a gold star right here on this page. Your "equipment" should consist of a nutcracker, a pick, a seafood fork, a fingerbowl, plenty of napkins, and a bib. Yes, a bib. My first real experience was in Newport, Rhode Island one summer on vacation. My family and I found a "real" seafood restaurant with "real" lobster, and the waitress brought us three bibs, and only one of us was seated in a high-chair! Right away I knew this would be a challenge. A lobster revolts at being your dinner right from the very beginning. He will sometimes spray water when cracked open. Carefully twist off large claws with your hands. Crack the claws with the nutcracker and pull the meat out with your pick. The larger pieces of meat in the body and tail are much easier to remove and should be eaten with a knife and fork. If a sauce is offered, use your fork for dipping. The greenish color in the lobster's middle is called "tamale" (liver), and the pinky-coral color is the roe. Both are considered real delicacies and should at least be tried. Enjoy!

Melon—Small cubes or balls may be eaten with your spoon. Watermelon is eaten with a fork, avoiding seeds with each fork full. If you do get one, swallow the fruit; then, discreetly expel the seed onto the fork and then place on edge of plate. If the watermelon is offered at a picnic, it is absolutely all-American to eat by holding wedges in your hand. However, a lady never engages in seed spitting contests!

Nachos—Eat as you would dips and crunchies.

Pasta or Spaghetti—Back in the "olden days" when there was only one shape of spaghetti noodle, there was only one acceptable way to eat it—wind it around your fork at a slant using your spoon as a prop, then bring a realistic amount up to your mouth using only the fork. Do not suck a wayward noodle back into your mouth with a loud slurp; gently help it with your fork. Spaghetti is not cut up unless for a small child. There are many spoon and fork-size pastas popular now, that are delicious and easy to eat.

Shish-Kabob—Carefully hold the end of the skewer with one hand and gently guide the food off with your fork with the other hand. Skewer should be placed on edge of plate. Cut and eat each piece as usual.

Shrimp—Small shrimp in a cocktail sauce are eaten whole with your seafood fork. Sitting around peeling and eating steamed shrimp with family and friends is a wonderful past time as well as a delicious treat that may be enjoyed with your fingers. A fingerbowl with lemon would be nice.

Sneezing—This is certainly a normal body function, and if you're like most of us, a sneeze will come on pretty suddenly. Simply turn away from your neighbors, and cover your mouth and nose with your napkin. Gesundheit!

Soup—Don't put too much in your soup spoon and make sure you work the spoon away from you and then up to your mouth. Never slurp and never blow on hot soup. Let it cool naturally. Please do not tilt the bowl to retrieve the last spoonful and never pick the bowl up and drink (exception: small oriental broth cups).

Tea Bag—When drinking hot tea, remove bag with spoon, gently pressing it against inside of cup before removing. Place tea bag on saucer next to cup.

Understanding Menus

The following terms are used in restaurants and in the menus you may be given to choose your meal from:

A la—a French term meaning "in the style of"

A la carte—dishes that have to be individually ordered, as distinct from a complete meal that usually includes an appetizer, salad, main course and dessert for one price

A la king—chopped food, usually chicken or turkey, in a cream sauce with sliced mushrooms and pimento

A la maison—in the style of the restaurant or the house specialty

A la mode—pie or dessert topped with a scoop of ice cream

Amandine—made or served with almond nuts

Au gratin—a dish that's browned in the oven or broiler, usually topped with buttered bread crumbs or grated cheese, or both

Au jus—food, usually roast beef, served in its own juices.

Butterfly—to split food down the center but not quite all the way through so that the two halves can be opened flat like butterfly wings; often done with large shrimp or a thick fillet of steak when ordered well done

Café au lait—coffee with cream or milk

Canapé—small toast pieces covered with food spread

Carte du jour—menu of the day

Cordon Bleu—filled with cheese, ham or Canadian bacon

Crêpe—thin French pancakes

Du jour—it means "of the day," like "soup du jour"

En brochette—food that is cooked on a skewer

En concatte—cooked in a casserole

Entrée—main dish

Flambé—desserts soaked in liquor and set ablaze; (it would be wise to make sure an adult knows you're doing this).

Fricassee—This describes chicken or small game that's cooked in a sauce, usually with vegetables, after first being cut up and browned.

Fromage—French word for cheese

Hors d'oeuvres—foods served as appetizers

Julienne—cut in thin strips

Marinate—to steep (soak) meat, fish, fowl, vegetables, or other food in a spicy or sweet liquid for several hours until the food absorbs the flavor

Poisson—French word for fish

Poulet—French word for chicken

Provençale—dishes that are served with garlic, onion, mushrooms, herbs, and olive oil.

Purée—to grind to paste either by pressing through a food mill or whirling in an electric blender

Ragout—a hearty brown stew, highly seasoned

Sautéed—fried in a small amount of hot fat

Soufflé—very light egg mixture, whipped until it's frothy, then baked until puffy.

Table d'hôte—one price for the entire meal

Veau—French word for veal

Viande—French word for meat

Volaille—French word for poultry

After reading these, the menu still may seem "Greek" to you. Most of these terms are from the French language. Menu terms in an Italian restaurant will probably be in

Italian. Some menus list English translations on the side.
If not, ask an adult at the table to interpret. When no adult
is present, simply smile and ask the waiter or waitress to
translate! If understanding is not the problem, but
pronouncing it is, simply lift your menu when the waiter
or waitress comes around, point to the "mystery dish" of
your choice and hope for the best! Ask for pronunciation
for future reference.

The Who's Who of Restaurants

You may already be familiar with some of the people
and what they do, but here's a short review in the order
that you may encounter them:

Maître d'—(pronounced may-treh-dee) is the head
waiter. The fancier the restaurant, the more elegantly he
will be dressed—a tuxedo perhaps. He's in charge of the
other waiters, and it is also his responsibility to see that
everyone is seated efficiently. If your family has a certain
restaurant that they go to on special occasions, you may
see your Dad "tip" the maître d' from time to time.
Perhaps your Mom has a favorite table at which to sit, and
your Dad wants to assure that it has been reserved for
you. The maître d' is usually very charming and friendly.
In some restaurants he may also be the manager or owner.

Hostess—If the restaurant is not quite as formal, there
will be a hostess to seat you and your family. She will
probably be the one to give you your menus as well. A
girl or woman always follows the hostess (or maître d')
to the table and the man follows behind the woman.

Waiter or Waitress—This person may wear a name tag
or introduce themselves to you by their first name. They
will take your order and serve your food. Be pleasant and
smile. This is not an easy job. Speak clearly and try not to
change your mind after placing the order. Should you
need the waiter's or waitress' assistance, do not call, "Hey
you," or "Boy," but "Waiter" or "Miss" if you cannot
remember their name. They receive a tip of 15 to 20
percent of the entire check total.

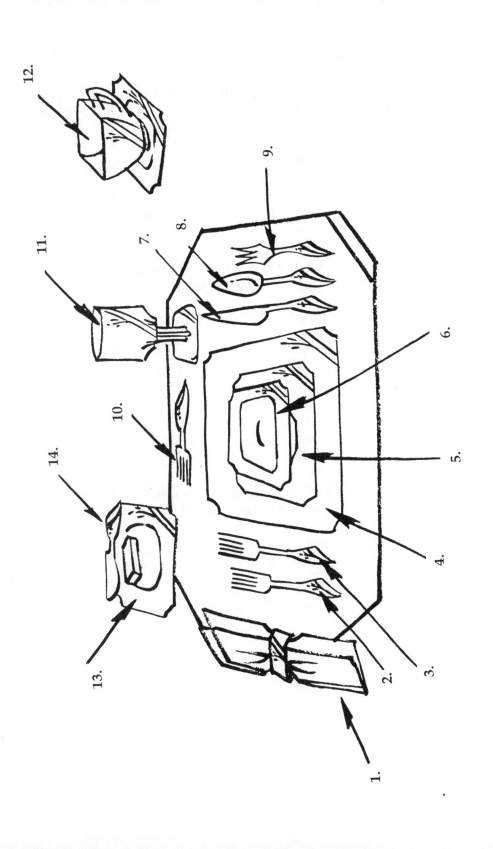

Busboy—This person is the waiter's or waitress' assistant. He will clear tables, bring water, and keep your table clean and orderly. Your waiter or waitress will split the tip from the check with him.

Restroom Attendant or Valet—In nicer restaurants, there may be a lady in the restroom to offer you fresh towels, hand lotion, etc. You will normally see restroom attendants in the evening hours. For tips on tipping, see Chapter 3.

Components of a Basic Table Setting
(See drawing on previous page.)

1. Napkin (and napkin ring, optional)
2. Salad Fork
3. Dinner Fork
4. Dinner Plate
5. Salad Plate
6. Soup Bowl
7. Dinner Knife
8. Soup Spoon
9. Seafood Fork
10. Dessert Fork
11. Water Goblet (wine goblet would be smaller, but matching and to the right of the water goblet)
12. Cup and Saucer
13. Bread and Butter Plate
14. Butter Spreader

Chapter 3
Tummy Churning Feats
Made Simple

If you'll think about it, the only time we really need to be nervous about doing something for the first time is when we're not prepared. Oh sure, a few butterflies are expected when we embark upon a new task or meet someone special for the first time, but half the battle is "doing your homework," as they say!

Your teen and in-between years are full of discoveries and new experiences. In this chapter we'll learn:

Introductions

How and when to tip

How to be a good house guest

Having a friend who is "different"

Traveling alone

Introductions

Executing a proper introduction can even give adults jiggly knees!

One of the nicest benefits of all the new self-confidence that you are gaining are the new friends you will meet. Some of them will be introduced to you by others; some you will go up to all by yourself and proudly announce, "Hi! I'm Elizabeth, the new girl in your science class. Do you sing int the chorus?"

There's no doubt that you will want all of these new friends to meet each other as well. Then, of course, you will want them to visit your home and meet your family. Oh; am I making it sound complicated? It doesn't have to be if you follow a few simple rules:

New friends first.

Ladies first.

Elders first.

Well, maybe it's not quite that simple, but it doesn't have to frighten you to the point that you just don't learn how to "share" all these new friends. That's right - share. Introducing someone you like to another person is just like sharing them! I don't know of a nicer gift to give - or to receive. Let's discuss some more of the "how-to's."

I am sure that most of you have made lots and lots of introductions without even knowing it. The last time a friend came home with you after school and you said, "Mom, this is Matt Michaels," that was an introduction. Remember to always speak so that others can hear you and understand you when you do an introduction. Sometimes people mumble when they are nervous or unsure of what they are supposed to say. Think about what you are going to say before you say it, and you won't have any problems.

I can't think of anything about doing introductions that can put butterflies in your stomach faster than forgetting someone's name. Most people have had that happen to them, and they will all tell you that just being honest is the best bet. When it happens to me, I just say, "Please refresh my memory. Your name has slipped my mind." That's really the best you can do and most people will understand. Many times I have the mothers of my Charm School students approach me in a shopping mall several years after their daughters have finished the class. I will probably always remember their face, but unless they tell me whose Mom they are, I will probably not recall their name. Be a good friend. Instead of standing there watching someone look for a hole to crawl into from embarrassment, help them out. I'm certain they will not forget your name again!

Basically, there are two ways to do introductions; formal and informal. The method you choose may depend on how old you are or where you are.

A sample of the informal way would be, "This is my friend, Erica Rawls." The same introduction done formally would be, "May I present my friend, Miss Erica Rawls." The "fancy" way might seem a little more adult, so make certain that the occasion calls for such an introduction. You wouldn't want your friends to think you are "putting on airs."

It is important to stand up when you are introducing or when you are being introduced. It not only shows respect, but shows that you are really interested in meeting the new friend. I always like to repeat the new person's name immediately. "Katie, I would like you to meet Ramona." It is helpful if I then say, "Ramona, it is so nice to meet you." Now I have had the chance to use her name while I am looking at her. It also helps some people to make a little mental picture in their mind of something about the new friend. We all have our own method to help us remember. There used to be page after page of strict rules for introducing new friends. If you stick to the basics, you won't have any problems. There are, however, some situations that may be a little more formal. Should you ever have the pleasure of meeting the President of the United States, you would say, "How do you do, Mr. President." If the special person was a King or Queen, you would say, "How do you do, Your Majesty."

In the rare (and exciting!) case of meeting royalty, a curtsey would be appropriate for young ladies of **all ages.** A curtsey looks a little like a bow and a little like a dance step. If you are wearing a skirt or dress, you delicately hold the sides of your skirt between your thumb and index finger. Take your right foot and draw an imaginary half-circle with your toe until it is directly behind the heel of your left foot. Pretend that there is a bucket of water on your head. Now if you tip your head, you are not only going to get water all over you, but all over the Queen! Practice in front of a mirror the next time you feel special.

Remember to smile not only when you are performing an introduction but when you are being introduced. It shows immediate friendship and will make the other person feel at ease instantly. Finally, look directly at the person when doing an introduction or when being introduced.

When a girl of age twelve or older is introduced to an older man, it is appropriate for her to extend her hand. If you were being introduced to an older woman, you should wait for her to extend her hand to you. Young girls rarely shake hands with each other. When you are much older it would not only be acceptable but considered proper business etiquette.

You will want to address most adults as "Miss," "Mr.," or "Mrs." Some single women that have been separated, divorced or widowed prefer to be addressed as "Ms."

It is considered improper for a young person to be too casual or too "familiar" with an adult's name or title. You would not refer to a teacher by his or her first name even if it were a teacher you felt especially close to.

Adults with special titles, jobs or positions are sometimes introduced or referred to in a special way:

THE MAYOR: "How do you do, Mr. Mayor" or "How do you do, Mayor Rodriequez."

THE RABBI: "How do you do, Rabbi Stein" or "How do you do, Rabbi."

PROTESTANT MINISTER: "How do you do, Rev. Rhodes" or "How do you do, Sir."

CATHOLIC PRIEST: "How do you do, Father Flanagan" or "How do you do, Father."

NUN: "How do you do, Sister" or "How do you do, Sister Maria."

THE GOVERNOR: "How do you do, Governor Roberts."

HIS WIFE: "How do you do, Mrs. Roberts."

A SENATOR: "How do you do, Senator Hackney" or "How do you do, Senator."

Introducing a boy to a girl - Say the girl's name first:

Phoebe Carlton, this is Andy Jones

Introducing a boy to your sister - Look first at your sister and say her name:

Ashley, this is Dale Dole

Then look back and say, Ashley is my sister.

Introducing a friend to your Mother - A boy looks at his Mom and says her name first:

Mom, this is Elizabeth Bouvier

Elizabeth, this is my Mom, Mrs. Andrew (especially helpful if your last name is different from your Mom's).

Introducing a man to a woman - You say the woman's name first:

Mrs. Kelly, this is Mr. Rydell

Introducing a person your age to an older person - You say the older person's name first:

Mr. Poe, this is Carissa Wells

Introducing any boy to your Dad - Say your Dad's name first:

Dad. this is Jamie Smith

Introducing a school-age girl to your Dad - Look first at your Dad and say his name:

Dad, this is Kristin Olsen

Introducing your brother to a boy - You look first at your friend and say his name:

Jerry Harris, this is my brother Jack

There you have it. Some easy examples to follow for introductions. As with all of the other new things your are learning, just remember that self confidence and a big smile can cover up minor mistakes and a case of the butterflies!

How and When To Tip

What's a tip? A tip is a monetary "thank you" to someone who performs a task or service. This tip is in addition to the initial payment for the goods, task or service. When you are served in a restaurant for example, you will be presented with a check (bill) after you eat. Your *tip* should be figured on the total amount of the check. Fifteen to twenty percent is customary. If the service provided by the restaurant and your server were exceptional, the tip should reflect that. The same holds true if the service was inferior. However, I do not believe that a small or non- existent tip should go un-mentioned. If the service that you or your party (group) received was that bad, the restaurant management should be told.

If the food and the service was wonderful, please don't be skimpy with your praise to the manager or Maitre d'. You may also choose to reflect this praise in your tip.

If your total check is $18.62:

your tip would be: 15% or $2.79 (good service)

to

$3.72 or 20% (excellent service)

Now, should you leave those pennies to make it exactly $2.79? No. Always round up for a tip. Therefore, $2.80 would be proper. If the restaurant is more formal (table linen, maitre d' etc.) I would suggest rounding up to the nearest dollar, making your tip $3.00 or $4.00 in the case of excellent service. If you gave your server a $20.00 bill with this check you would receive $1.38 change. You could add the additional money to the tip after your change is returned or preferably add the additional $.62 or so to it when paying your server and quietly thank them and say, "no change will be necessary."

Restroom Valet or Attendant - The customary tip is $.25 - $.50 during the day, $.75 - $1.00 in the evening.

Maitre d' - Adults will sometimes "cross the palm" of the maitre d' in their favorite restaurants with "folding money" (bills only) for holding a reservation or preparing their favorite table.

Porter - The **porter** who carries your baggage from a taxi to hotel door, terminal to car, etc., should receive $.50 per bag as minimum. The porter or room steward on a train with sleeping cars or cruise ship is tipped for carrying baggage, making beds, etc. at the end of the trip. Several dollars per day would be acceptable.

Airline Host or Hostess - (Flight Attendant or Stewardess) No tip is expected, but excellent manners, courtesy and "Thank yous" are!

Being a House Guest

What a treat! You've been invited to spend the night with a classmate or perhaps an entire weekend with an out-of-town friend.

1. Be sure that both parents or other adult in charge say it's okay. Quite often, overnight plans are made during school on Friday, only to discover that families have made other plans. That can really be disappointing.

2. Don't pack everything you own. Don't give Michelle's mom the idea that you've moved in for good! For overnight neighborhood type sleep-overs, one tote bag with the basics is all you will need: toothbrush, PJ's, change of play clothes, and anything else special you would need for additional activities. If you're going somewhere with your friend's entire family, make sure you know how much money you might need to take with you, and be certain to let your family know exactly where you'll be.

3. For longer visits, you'll need an ample supply of clothing (underwear too), shampoo, conditioner, tampons and any other personal items you may need so that you won't have to borrow things unless it's absolutely necessary.

4. Don't criticize the way your friend's family does things. Don't complain and say things like, "My Mom doesn't make me do that." For a short time, you can adjust to things done a different way.

5. Offer to help around the house. Don't scatter your belongings all over, and don't act as though you're there to be waited on.

6. What a great opportunity to try out some new foods! Don't say, "Yuc, my Mom never makes us eat that!" Say, "No, thank you" or better yet, try a little!

7. For sleep-overs at a classmates house in your neighborhood, a short thank you note should be written the first time you spend the night. After that, a sincere "Thank you, Mrs. Wilder. I had a wonderful time," is adequate.

8. For weekend visits (or longer), a lovely thank you letter mailed *as soon* as you are home, as well as a small token gift is in order. Perhaps some potpourri or some scented soaps. The gift should have been purchased ahead of time, wrapped and brought with you so that you may leave it before you depart.

9. Lastly, but absolutely not least - DON'T SNOOP!

Having a Friend Who Is Different

Just as some of us are thin and some of us are a little lumpier than others, friends come in all sorts of "packages." Growing up with a disability is a lot different than it used to be. When I was in elementary school there was a "special" class. The kids in that class are mentally retarded - and they were verbally terrorized each and every day as they proudly marched to the cafeteria to join the rest of us. Their painful expressions seemed to say, "Please be my friend and play."

Much progress has been made in recent years as students with both mental and physical disabilities are *mainstreamed* into regular school classes.

I have worked with the Easter Seal Society for many years, both as a volunteer and for a while as a Director. The one message that repeats itself over and over from kids, teens and adults with disabilities is "Respect me and treat me the same way you want to be treated."

One way that we can accomplish this is to not categorize or "group" individuals with disabilities. Never say "the handicapped," "the crippled children...," "the disabled," or "the afflicted," as if they belong on another planet!

The boy down the street who has Down Syndrome or the girl in the wheelchair with Spina Bifida are just like you. They like neat clothes, great music and being silly with their friends sometimes.

Remember, it's okay to ask questions. Most teens I know with disabilities would not be insulted if you asked an honest question or two. "Can you go camping?" "How do you dance?"

The greatest gift you could give yourself or a person your age with a disability is friendship. You have my guaranteed reward of a "warm fuzzy" feeling!

For more information on how you can make a difference for kids and teens in you community with disabilities, contact your local Easter Seal Society or write to the National Easter Seal Society at:

The Easter Seal Society
70 East Lake Street
Chicago, Illinois 60601

Traveling Alone

The first time I traveled alone was in my junior year of High School. I had been selected to compete for the title of "Miss Junior Achievement" at the J.A. National Convention. I don't know which I was more nervous of - traveling alone or the competition!

The key to traveling alone without trauma is careful planning prior to your trip. Your parents will probably do this for you whether you'll travel by air, train or bus there are a few helpful hints to assure this first excursion into the big, real world will be an exciting one.

* Review all details of your trip with an adult before departure. If you have tickets make sure you know exactly how to read them. Airline tickets can be particularly confusing the first time.

* Dress comfortably - but neatly.

* Take as few pieces of luggage as possible. Remember that "carry-on" baggage must fit under you seat or in designated compartments that are not very large. Also make sure that all pieces of your luggage are identified with your name and address.

* Be aware of your schedule. If you need to change flights or get on a different bus or train make sure you're not snoozing or mesmerized by a good novel!

* Wear a watch and watch the time.

* Have change for telephone calls and all pertinent phone numbers available.

* Don't be afraid to ask questions. "Where's the terminal?" "Do I keep my ticket stub?"

* Have cash, travelers checks or a credit card with you for emergencies.

* Don't be fooled by thinking you have extra time to explore the scenery while waiting in a terminal or waiting station. Stay where the majority of people are waiting. There will be plenty of opportunities to explore when you have reached your exciting destination!

In conclusion, just remember that you need only do what you do with confidence. Common sense and the ability to treat others as you wish to be treated. The rest comes with experience - and I know that all of your new experiences will be exciting ones!

Chapter 4.
Garbage In...Garbage Out

*If I am constantly aware of what
goes in my mouth,
My hips will not be likely to spread
from North to south!*

Ahh—youth. When I was sixteen I could eat a bag of corn chips, several colas and chase it down with some chocolate and still be in my "skinny pants" for Friday night.

Now please understand. I'm not saying that I ate like that very often—but what's an occasional pajama party without breaking out massive doses of junk food! Far be it from me to abstain!

I suppose one of the virtues of age is intelligence. But, one of the realities of age is that what you eat makes a more noticeable difference once you've cruised through your teen years. Your metabolism and your body's ability to burn calories often slow down as you become older. The gooey chocolate eclair you could eat with no consequences at fifteen may sit on your hips virtually overnight by the age of thirty!

That's why it's so important to establish smart eating habits while you still have youth on your side.

In this chapter we'll discuss how your body turns food into beauty power, how to deal with being overweight and how to eat healthier.

Understanding Your Beauty Factory

Beauty is an Inside Job.

As soon as you put food in your mouth, your digestive system starts to work! Chewing your food is the first step, so you can send small pieces (not chunks!) down to your stomach. Your stomach breaks food into very small portions and then sends it to the small intestine where final digestion occurs. "Good Nutrition" is absorbed through the small intestine. Any food that is not digested by the time it leaves the small intestine goes into the large intestine, or colon. The colon is the body's garbage dump.

56

Maintaining good colon health is very important to keep your body healthy and vibrant.

The stomach, and large and small intestine are the central parts of your digestive system. Just as important though are the pancreas, gallbladder and the liver which assist digestion with special and very necessary enzymes.

The foods you eat affect how well your digestive system works. Eating too many foods that are high in fat, sugar, sodium, alcohol and caffeine, to mention a few culprits, forces your digestive system to work overtime.

After too many years of constant overtime, your digestive system will not perform well! Eating good wholesome foods helps your digestive system work at top form which leads to good health.

Growing Up Overweight

Growing up as an overweight teen can be a traumatic experience. Growing up "different" in any way is no "picnic"—but being too heavy can rob you of your self—confidence as well as your energy and productivity.

Eating habits are formed at an early age and when you're young you really have no choice but to eat what is provided for you. However, you can make suggestions to your Mom when she goes to the market. Ask her to buy fruits, raw veggies, and yogurt for example, and leave the cookies at the store.

If you were overweight as a child, you will probably be an overweight teen and the chances are good that you will be an overweight adult. It's so much easier to lose weight when you're young. Chances are you're more active than someone three or four times your age, (although not necessarily!)

I've seen too many overweight teens who lacked self-confidence and missed out on some of life's special activities as a result. A dear friend of mine in her early twenties who I'll call "Madeline" has had a weight problem all of her life. We've all referred to an overweight friend as having, "a good personality and such a pretty face." But, no truer words have ever been spoken. This girl is one of the sharpest, most beautiful I know. She was also very short and had a very large bust—making her look even heavier. She had breast reduction surgery, lost a few pounds, but nothing monumental. Then she fell in love. The young man she fell in love with was equally as heavy as she so there went Madeline's incentive. On top of that she became pregnant. Long story made short—the husband is out of the picture, her beautiful child is a joy. She has lost enormous amounts of weight and has a wonderful new job and a social life that I simply cannot keep track of! But, the real treat is that she is discovering what all of us knew all along—she is wonderful and has so much to offer. Now that the "excess baggage" is out of the way she is able to cultivate her self-confidence as well as her many other attributes.

Remember, if you're trying to lose weight please do it sensibly. Sensible eating and a regular exercise program must be used jointly. Gimmicks and "Get Thin Quick" programs are a waste of time and money. Do it right and do it while you are young.

I've run into girls I went to school with that are twenty to thirty pounds overweight, have two or three children and will tell you, "I just never lost the baby weight." That simply does not have to happen. I weigh less now than before I had my first child. No—I don't run marathons or starve myself. I am realistic about what I do and I stay healthy—both in body and in spirit. It's a package deal and I want your whole "package" to be one that you're proud of. Read on.

"I'll Just Grab Something Quick & Easy"

We live in an age of quick and easy. We often think we've got it so rough. Rush, rush, rush all the time. School, sports, music, dance, scouting, babysitting, dating. When do you have time for *you*?

Have you ever eaten "fast food"? Most of you are answering "yes" to this question. When something is quick and easy we often must sacrifice nutritional value.

In all fairness, that's not always the case. Most of the national fast food restaurant chains have yielded to consumer pressure in recent years and are using less animal fats and less added salt. You need to be aware of the nutritional content of the burgers, fries and other foods that have become an American staples. Most of us indulge occasionally in "fast food" and there's really no harm done. Problems in nutritional balance occur when "fast food" routinely takes the place of traditionally prepared meals.

The lists and tips that follow are included as a quick and easy reference for your use.

It's not just how much you eat, how many calories or how many grams of carbohydrates that matter. It's *what* you eat that makes such a difference.

For example:

Food Choice	Calories (g)	Fat (g)	Cholesterol (mg)	Sodium (mg)
Burger King				
Whopper Sandwich with cheese	706	44	115	1177
*Medium Fries (salted)	341	20	21	241
Chocolate Shake	326	10	31	198
Garden Salad (without dressing)	95	5	15	125
McDonald's				
Big Mac	570	35	83	979
Chicken McNuggets (3.8 oz)	323	21.3	73	512
Apple Pie (3 oz)	253	14.3	12	398
Egg McMuffin (4.9 oz)	340	15.8	259	885
Wendy's				
Broccoli & Cheese Baked Potato	500	25.0	22	430
Chicken Sandwich on a Wheat Bun	320	10.0	59	500

* Cooked in 100 percent vegetable oil
Please Note: Nutritional guides are yours for the asking at any national "convenience food chain."

Some Healthy Choices

Instead of...	**Have...**
Candy bar	Frozen Banana
Creamed soups	Broth or consomme
White bread	Whole wheat or whole grain bread
Whole or 2% milk	1% or skim milk
Fried foods	Baked or broiled selections
Salt	Lemon juice, pepper, spices
Butter	Margarine
Sour cream	Plain low-fat yogurt
Ice cream	Frozen low-fat yogurt
Tuna in oil	Tuna in water
Cookies for snacks	Fresh fruit
Deep fried vegetables	Steamed vegetables

Some Healthy Snacks
1 plain baked potato (3-4 oz.)
1 slice whole wheat bread
1 peach
1/2 cantaloupe
1 small raw apple
1 ounce raisins
1 banana
15 grapes
1 orange or tangerine
1/2 cup high fibre cereal with skim milk
1/2 cup low-fat cottage cheese
1 small container low-fat yogurt
1/2 grapefruit
1 small bowl of lettuce with low-fat vinaigrette
Cucumber slices
Plain popcorn
Rice cakes with low-fat cream cheese
Carrot sticks
Celery sticks with peanut butter

Some Healthy—Helpful Hints
* Eat slowly—you'll become full without over-eating.
* Use smaller plates to create an illusion of more food. It's psychological—but it works.
* Eat snacks with a lot of crunchiness.
* Participate in a healthy physical activity 3 to 5 times per week for at least 20 minutes each time.
* Walk whenever possible. Take the stairs in place of elevators and escalators when you can.
* Visualize yourself at the weight you desire. Tape a picture of someone you admire and would like to emulate in a prominent place (like the inside of your locker).
* Drink 6 to 8 glasses of water per day. It makes you feel fuller, it's healthy and it's great for keeping your skin soft and your hair shiny.

Some Healthy Calorie Burning Activities

Activity	Approximate Calories Per Hour
Roller skating	350
Walking (rapidly)	400
Swimming (average speed)	600
Golfing	250
Bicycling (average speed)	350
Fast Dancing	400
Ice Hockey	550
Tennis	400
Running	920
Writing at your desk	20 (oh well)
Calisthenics	300
Cross-country skiing	600
Gardening	150

Healthful eating begins with the four food groups concept:

Vegetables and Fruit Group

4 servings per day

Citrus fruit, tomatoes, dark green or yellow vegetables and canned fruits

Bread and Cereal Group

4 servings per day

Bread, cooked cereal, tortillas, rice or ready-to-eat cereal

Milk and Cheese Group

3 to 4 servings per day

Milk, yogurt, cheese, cottage cheese, ice-cream or ice-milk

Meat and Poultry Group

2 servings per day

Meat, poultry, eggs, cooked dry beans or peas, peanut butter or nuts

Note:Balance these four groups so you eat about 2/3 of your calories from the first two groups (complex carbohydrates) about 1/3 from the last two groups (fat and protein).

A Guide to Vitamins and Minerals

Vitamin	Will help my body to:	I will need to eat:
A	- have healthy skin - have good eyesight - have strong bones and teeth	Liver, egg yolks, leafy green vege-tables, whole milk, cheese, butter, sweet potatoes, apricots
D	- use calcium and phosphorus to build strong bones and teeth	Whole milk, oily fish, egg yolk, (and a moderate amount of sun-light on skin)

Vitamin	Will help my body to:	I will need to eat:
E	- use vitamins A and C better - prevent cell damage	Wheat germ oil, vegetable oils, green vegetables, nuts, margarine
K	- keep blood healthy; aids in normal clotting	Liver, egg yolk, kale, lettuce, spinach, cabbage
C	- help hold body cells together - help in healing of wounds and broken bones - help body resist infection - keep gums and teeth healthy	Citrus fruits and juices, strawberries, cantaloupe, tomatoes, broccoli, green vegetables, potatoes
Thiamin	- turn carbohydrates into energy - keep nervous system healthy	Whole grain breads and cereals, pork, liver, poultry, fish, peanuts
Riboflavin (B2)	- use proteins, fats and carbohydrates to produce energy and build tissue - maintain healthy facial skin and eyes	Milk and milk products, meat, liver, eggs, green leafy vegetables, breads and cereals
Niacin (B3)	- use carbohydrates for energy - use oxygen to relieve energy - keep nervous system healthy	Fish, poultry, meats, whole grain or enriched breads, nuts
B6	- use protein - forming red blood cells - use body fat for energy	Pork, liver, cereal, poultry, fish, spinach
B12	- produce red blood cells - keep nervous system healthy - build new protein	Liver, kidney, meat, fish, milk, eggs

Vitamin	Will help my body to:	I will need to eat:
Folacin	- produce red blood cells - use carbohydrates, fats and protein	Liver, legumes, green leafy vegetables
Biotin	- use proteins, fats and carbohydrates properly	Liver, egg yolks, dark green vegetables,

Healthy Body...Healthy Mind

Some girls (and adults) always feel like they are too heavy no matter what size they are. They are so terrified by gaining weight that they will either try to starve themselves or eat very little. We call this condition *anorexia nervosa*.

Other people appear on the surface to be eating normally, but will make themselves vomit after each meal just to make sure they won't gain weight. We call this condition *bulimia*.

Both of these conditions can be very dangerous—even fatal. Individuals with these conditions will never think they are thin enough—no matter how thin they are.

I know of several girls who ultimately were hospitalized as a result of eating disorders. What follows does not conjure up a very pretty sight. One girl told me of a tube that was inserted down her nose while another was nourished intravenously (through a needle placed underneath the skin through which liquid nourishment flows).

Please have the courage to talk to your parents or another adult whom you trust if you suspect any problem—especially one of these very serious eating disorders.

In a world that stresses beauty and perfection in so many aspects of life, it may seem difficult to be less than **your** image of perfection.

If you are afraid to talk to your parents or another adult, call a telephone operator for information about health counseling services in your community. You deserve to feel good about yourself. There are people available to help you.

Learn to read food packages. The knowledge available to you from sources such as labeling, nutritional guides and magazines are extremely beneficial.

In addition to the physical benefits of proper nutrition, there are psychological ones, too. You'll feel better about yourself, the way you look and the things you do. The satisfaction of achieving a goal will boost your self-confidence.

Remember to budget your nutritional needs the way you'd budget your allowance. If you needed twenty dollars to get a sweater out of layaway, you wouldn't spend all of your babysitting money on nail polish. If you're attending a dessert buffet on Saturday, you'd probably want to pass up chocolates on Friday.

Just remember to use your head before you using your mouth (not just when selecting foods!) to ensure good health that lasts a lifetime.

III.

The Best Outer Me Make-over

Chapter 5
Fitness ... While It's Still Easy

What does it mean to you when I say, "Claire is poised?"

Do you get a mental picture of someone who is self-confident, has good posture, doesn't make jerky or nervous movements? Your should, because *poise* is the special language that our body silently speaks to others. If I am standing with my arms folded across my chest and tapping my foot, do I look happy and carefree? No, I look impatient. You instantly know what's on my mind. Do your parents have a special "body language" that tells what their mood is? I'll bet they do. You probably know what they're upset about before they say one word!

Your mannerisms, walk, gestures and just about everything else you do with your body will be an indication of how much "poise" or self-confidence you have.

There may be times when you feel that you are "all arms and legs." This is perfectly normal because until your are fifteen or sixteen years old, various arts of the body grow at different rates at different times.

These changes can make a girl feel awkward and ugly—but actually, you're growing prettier. Just remember that most things that are really worth having don't appear overnight but are nurtured and gently cared for with understanding and patience. Your body is no different.

Poise is simply that special way you carry yourself. It's the difference between dragging your feet and shuffling over to sit in a chair and holding your head high while you ease effortlessly toward your destination.

It is the efficient use of your body's movement. Once you are able to move about gracefully, being "poised" will simply be second nature to you. You'll find that you won't even have to concentrate on how to do these things. Then you'll be free to devote all of your attention to more important things—like making new friends and learning new and wonderful things in the world around you!

The proper beginning for doing everything with poise is having good posture. When you stand up straight and tall, you have good posture, and your body will be properly aligned—or "stacked up."

1. Your chin will be parallel with the floor (not pointing up or down).

2. Your earlobes will be placed directly over your shoulders.

3. Your shoulders will be held back, but not rigid.

4. Your tummy will be tucked in, even if you don't have one!

5. Your bottom will be tucked under (no swaybacks, please).

6. Your arms should be relaxed at your side.

7. Your knees should be straight but not locked.

8. Last, but *super* important, is what we do with our feet. It's called a *Basic Stance.*

The *Basic Stance* looks a little like the letter "T"; therefore, some people call it a "Basic T" or a "Model's T."

That's what it looks like, but what it *looks* like, but what it *does* is give you a nifty little way to stand so that you'll always look calm, cool and collected! That could really come in handy during a presentation, don't you think?

A basic stance also looks a little like 2:00 on the face of a clock. The left foot would be the hour hand pointing straight up at the "12" and the right foot would be the minute had directed at the "2."

The left foot is the "front" foot and the right foot is the "back" foot. Be certain to settle the weight of your body onto your back foot so that you won't be leaning forward. When you walk out of a basic stance, you would always use the front foot. Why? That's right. If you try to walk on the back foot , you'll trip a little because you'll need to shift your weight again. It's easy—front foot first—the foot that's all set to go and pointing straight ahead.

I'll bet you never thought that anyone would make up rules for learning how to walk. You learned how to do it when you were just a baby, didn't you! Well, just think of this as the "new and improved" method! Everything you will learn in this book, although some of it may be a little different from what you've done before, is meant to make your life easier and happier.

Now that you're standing properly, lets do a few exercises to be certain that your posture remains perfect.

Stand up against the wall with the heel of your back foot against the wall. Take your hand and see if it will fit between the wall and your waistline. Is there a big gap? Your hand should just barely fit without lots of extra space. If there is a lot of room left, bend your knees and slowly begin to dip down, keeping your hand behind your back. About half way down, you'll notice that the space between you and the wall has disappeared. Of course, you can't walk away from the wall in a squatting position just to have a straight back, but it really is a great way to remind yourself of what good posture should feel like.

The same exercise can be done lying on a flat surface but instead of gliding down a wall, you simply draw your knees up toward your hips, keeping your feet flat on the floor.

When I first began these exercises, I think you could have driven a truck under my back, but after several weeks of practice, practice, practice, I could just barely wedge my hand in—and the results are beautiful when you proudly walk away.

Have A Seat, Please

You're going to look super while you're standing, but eventually you'll need to pull up a chair—or actually walk over to one. Stand so that your feet are in the *Basic Stance* with your back leg touching the front of the chair. Now, place your hands on the front of your thighs to help you keep your balance. Bend your knees, and with your back perfectly straight, lower yourself onto the edge of the chair but don't "melt" into it. if your feet still reach the floor, either keep them in the *Basic Stance* or cross your ankles. Fold your hands gracefully and put in your lap, resting *on* your left leg (never wedged between your legs, as your knees will push apart! Horrors!)

To stand up, simply reverse the steps, keeping your back straight and your head held high.

These sitting and standing hints will really come in handy the next time you are any place where the eyes are on you!

Floating Through Air

Now that you're almost finished reading this chapter, you can use this book for something else for a while. Have you ever heard of anyone waking with a book on their head? Don't laugh—it's really lots of fun. Place your book on top of your head and don't let go until it feels secure. Now, place your hands down at your side and walk out of your basic stance with your front foot slowly and carefully. We're not running a race—just practicing the regal walk of a princess.

This procedure—although it may make you feel a little self-conscious—is the tried and true method for teaching young girls (and fashion models) the prettiest way to get from one point to another.

Please practice with shoes on, not sneakers, but a shoe with a smooth bottom. It's easier to walk on wood, tile or linoleum. Carpet makes your feet a little sluggish.

Okay, you're walking along and need to turn and go in the opposite direction. What do you do? A *pivot*.

Pivoting simply means turning around, and yes, you've probably been doing it for years without knowing it.

1. Stand with feet in *basic stance* position. The front foot is pointed straight ahead toward your audience.

2. Pick up front foot as if you were going to take a step.

3. Bring your back foot up now, and turn on the balls of your feet. If your *left* foot was your first foot, pivot to the *right*. If it's the *right* foot, pivot to the *left*.

4. There! You did it!

A Few More Poise Pointers

* If you must open a door to exit one room and enter another, be certain to turn around and face in the direction of the group you are leaving, smile and acknowledge them as you shut the door in front of you.

* Never straddle a beach towel as you prepare to lower yourself onto the sandy beach as you will form a very alarming view of yourself from the rear! Simply kneel down next to the towel, lower yourself onto your side, and then get situated. Much nicer!

* When picking objects off the floor, always bend from your knees—never lean straight over—not attractive and certainly not very good for your back.

* Never crawl onto the seat of a car, but lower yourself onto the edge of the seat and swing your legs up and over into the car, keeping your knees together at all times. (Teeny-tiny cars and vans and trucks take a little practice.

* Just remember—everything you do is part of the "puzzle,"—the puzzle of helping you to be the very best you that you can be.

Chapter 7

Skin "Care"ful

If you're like most girls I know you've already flipped past this chapter to chapter eight. After all, isn't sitting down with a full palette of fun eyeshadow colors a lot more fun than a detailed explanation of blackheads? Don't answer that!

Well, there **are** times when being practical takes over. This is one such time. All of the expensive make-up in the world cannot "make-up" for beautiful healthy skin. You'll thank me one day. I promise.

Proper skin care procedures should begin long before they are visibly necessary. If you're still twelve or thirteen and acne or oil hasn't yet become a factor, it may seem unnecessary to spend any extra time on your crystal clear skin. But, "bad skin" doesn't happen overnight. Problems with your skin are determined by several factors:

* Personal Hygiene
* Diet
* Exercise
* Environment

The most important one is your overall health. Have you ever noticed that your skin looked dull or pale when you were sick? Does your skin ever show the effects of too many late nights without removing make-up? How about the effects of poor diet? Any of these factors can practically guarantee you a less than perfect complexion.

Cleanliness is the most important part of any skin care routine. Now, when we speak of skin care, we are usually referring to the part of your skin found on your face. But you and I know that your skin is actually the largest body organ we have. It serves as our "air conditioner" and "filter." It protects us from the elements - *and* keeps all of your insides in!

Bubble baths probably rate very highly with most of you for fun ways to stay clean. There's hardly anything more lady-like and luxurious than a long, lazy bubble bath. It's also an excellent place to use your nail brush on your finger nails, toenails, elbows and heels. When you get out of the tub, smooth on an after-bath lotion. Apply it while skin is still warm and slightly damp. Now is a good time to fluff on lots of wonderful dusting powder!

If you're like most girls, you will need to choose a shower over a bath most of the time because showers take less time. It may just be too hectic around your house before school to take a bubble bath and tie up the bathroom for the needed amount of time. (After all, you shouldn't rush a bubble bath!) Choose one night per week for your special session - maybe Saturdays.

Facial Skin Care

There's no doubt that the portion of skin we all pay more attention to is under our hair line. That's right. It's that great face of yours! It is unique to you, and no one can be exactly like you.

When you take your daily bath or shower, you may also wash your face. A good habit to establish would be setting aside a different wash cloth or sponge just for your face and neck. *Actually*, a clean wash cloth should be used each time you wash your face, but your mother will probably scream when you tell her this. Solution: offer to wash and dry them yourself or use a facial sponge instead. Because the sponge is porous and dries quickly, germs and bacteria do not have an opportunity to grow. That's when you run into skin problems. Wash cloths normally get balled up (still drippy) and stuck in the corner of the bath tub. Then, while you're at school, they get warm and smelly - just the ideal environment for a new crop of "beasties" to jump back on your face next time you wash. Yuk!

Different skin types are similar to different hair types: normal, oily, dry, combination and problem. Remember that if you are under thirteen, or haven't started menstruation, you may not notice a certain "type" of skin yet. Just keeping it clean is the most important thing to do. Wash in the morning and again before bedtime using gentle circular motions with your cloth or sponge and a facial soap or cleansing solution.

It is important to know what type of skin you have so that you can take care of it properly and so you know what kind of make-up to choose.

Normal Skin

* Not too dry, not too oily
* Pores (your skin's "breathing holes") are practically invisible
* Not overly sensitive to products
* Cleanse with mild soap morning and night; rinse and pat dry with clean towel
* In cold weather, moisturize with a light lotion or cold cream on any exposed skin to avoid wind burn and chapping

Oily Skin

* Surface sometimes shiny with blackheads, pimples and large pores
* Wash with medicated soap morning and evening; rinse with warm water, then cool; pat dry
* If needed, apply mild astringent in "T-zone" (across forehead, down to nose and including chin); also, place on any other breakout points
* Never squeeze or pop a pimple; you can cause a scar and scars are forever. General rule is to not pick at your face ever!
* Apply light, non-oily moisturizer on flaky areas or if skin dries out in cold weather

Dry Skin

* Feels tight shortly after washing
* May sunburn easily
* Flakes and chaps easily

* Wash with creamy soap or gentle cleanser morning and night, rinse thoroughly; as leftover soap dries skin, pat dry
* Moisturize with non-oily, light weight cream morning and night; carry a sample size bottle with you for extra help during the day if needed

Combination Skin

* Some areas are dry, some oily, and some normal (T-zone is oily, rest is dry or normal)
* Cleanse with mild soap, rinse with warm water
* Apply mild astringent on oily areas, non-oily moisturizer to others

Problem Skin

* Often oily, may see frequent blackheads and enlarged pores
* Cleanse as often as needed with medicated soap, rinse with cool water, pat dry. Use medicated toner or astringent. Use acne medication if advised by dermatologist. - Keep hair "squeaky" clean, as dirt and oil in hair around face can increase problems on skin
* Keep hands just as clean, and do not pick at your face

To Tan or Not to Tan

Beware soft skinned beauties! Yes, **you**. This warning applies to each and every one of you. Those wonderful, warm, lazy days of summer seem to call us to the beach for fun and frolic - and no one will disagree with the fun factor! Just remember that even on a cloudy day the ultraviolet rays from the sun can beam down through the clouds and give you a nasty burn.

Your skin's production of "melanin" - a pigment released into the skin to naturally protect you from the sun - determines how easily you will tan. Too much of a good thing can be harmful. A sunscreen protects your skin and allows you to stay outside longer. If the sunscreen says that it has a SPF-8 (Sun Protection Factor), you can wear it and say outside eight times longer than with no protection. If you are very fair skinned, you may want to use a total sun block which does not allow any of the ultraviolet rays through. Remember that you will need to reapply the sunscreen product if you're perspiring or have just come out of the pool or ocean.

Although America's obsession with sun-bronzed bodies has produced many a handsome and beautiful tan, doctors have proved that these coppery exteriors are a breeding ground for skin cancer time bombs.

It will take many years of re-education before the message of "Pale is Pretty" hits home. You would have never seen Scarlett O'Hara with a tan, but by the mid 1920's it was all the rage. A suntan meant that you were wealthy enough to relax and play while the working class worked. Tanning *does* give you a healthy glow - but if all you need is the glow why not try one of the new instant bronzers on the market. I have tried both the over-night versions and the *truly* instant lotions. Personally I preferred the instant variety because I knew immediately how dark it would be and could guard against streaking. These should always be tested on a small patch of skin to determine any product sensitivity.

Preventing sun damage when you are young is the key to preventing skin cancer.

Please consider these ten factors that may put you in risk of contracting skin cancer.

1. Fair skin or freckles
2. Blonde, red or light brown hair
3. A tendency to burn easily and to tan little or not at all
4. Tendency to burn before finally tanning
5. A family history of skin cancer
6. Residing in a warm, sunny climate
7. Long periods of daily exposure to the sun

8. Short periods of intense exposure to the sun

9. A large number of moles (don't forget the ones you cannot easily see)

10. Repeated sunning without a sun screen

Look at fashion magazines. There is certainly no shortage of articles proclaiming the dangers of excess exposure to the sun, however the same magazine may also feature advertisements or fashion layouts depicting sun-bronzed beauties. I know this can be confusing. Many fashion photographers and magazine editors will insist that chalky white skin does not photograph as evenly as darker skin - and they are right to some extent. I have, however, noticed that many suntan products are showing their models skin several shades lighter than in the 1970's and early 1980's when sun screens were not nearly as prevalent.

Just remember, wrinkles are the least of your worries when the sun severely damages your skin. Play it safe!

Last, but certainly not least important; report any changes in a mole to a doctor, as well as any new lesions or patches of red inflamed skin.

How Your Skin is Constructed

This outer package called skin seems so simple, yet serves many purposes. Your skin:

* protects your body's nerves, glands and blood vessels
* protects your body from injury and infection
* serves as the "thermostat" that regulates you body temperature

Most of us never think about how complex our skin really is. We take for granted that it simply covers our lovely faces. A little science lesson - your skin is comprised of two layers:

1. EPIDERMIS - is the outer layer, the cellular part. The cells in the outermost layer of the epidermis die daily and fall off. Following a dedicated skin care program keeps these dead cells from lingering around and giving your skin a dull, leathery appearance. A weekly masque or facial can do wonders as extra help.

2. DERMIS - is the lower layer containing blood vessels and most of your nerve endings. It nourishes the outer layer with its oil glands and sweat glands. The oil glands keep your skin soft and pliable while the sweat glands serve as the skin's "air conditioner" and purifier.

3. SUBCUTANEOUS TISSUE - is found below the dermis and epidermis. This layer of fatty tissue protects as well as shapes and contours our skin. This layer thins as we age, and therefore can cause the skin to appear loose and saggy.

Skin is pretty marvelous. It's your body's largest functioning organ. It's your heating system. Your air conditioner and your safety vault! Now you see why it's so important to treat it with plenty of "T.L.C."

Your skin will probably change several times as you grow older. Typically, our skin is normal when we're very young, starts to get oily into our pre-teen and teen years, may be problem prone in our teens, continues to change and become combination in our twenties and thirties and will probably become fairly dry as we become much older.

You'll see and hear these words many times once you begin a skin care regimen.

Astringent - Product containing alcohol that helps to tighten and contract the pores.

Acid Mantle - Film of fluid that protects the skin from bacteria.

Freshener or Toner - Product containing less alcohol

than astringent (or perhaps none). Helps to remove any dirt or make- up left after cleansing.

P.H. Balance - Indicates the level of acidity or alkalinity in a product. A neutral level is 7.0 for skin care, cosmetics and hair products to be in balance with the levels in your body.

Pores - Tiny openings in the skin through which fluids may be discharged or absorbed.

Skin Care Fact or Fiction

Fiction	Fact
If my face breaks out this summer I'll just bake in the sun. That always clears up pimples!	A golden glow may temporarily camouflage the problem, but the sun will activate oil production causing more severe problems. Don't forget the damage factor.
Don't use a moisturizer if you have oily skin - that would just make it greasier.	Moisture and oil are two entirely different things. Use a non-comedogenic moisturizer (won't clog pores) to hydrate your skin without oil.
Oily, acne-prone skin needs to be scrubbed with soap and water frequently.	Aggressive cleansing can over-stimulate your oil glands signaling them to produce even more oil.
Falling asleep with your make-up on is okay as long as you wash it off in the morning.	Just one night of the "lazies" can give you a whole crop of "beasties." Skin must be cleansed morning and evening to assure proper hydration, rejuvenation and protection.

Skin Care "Never Never" Land

Never forget how much your diet affects the condition of your skin

Never tug, rub, pull or pinch your skin. Facial muscles stretch very easily and sagging can begin prematurely.

Never use a perfumed or deodorant soap on your face.

Never forget to protect and "shield" your skin with a moisturizer containing sunscreen.

Skin Care Extra Help

Once a week or once a month, turn a treatment into a treat with one of these:

Scrubs: Complexion polishers that keep skin free of debris by removing dead skin cells and unclogging pores. (should be avoided by those with extremely dry skin and surfaced pimples)

Facials: The at-home variety is easy. Bring a pot of water to a boil. Make a "tent" with a towel and hold your face above the steam for three to five minutes. While your pores are opened from the warm steam cleanse gently. Be careful not to get too close to the steam or let the towel touch the stove. Then, rinse with cool water to close pores and apply a moisturizer. Beauty-spa pampering doesn't have to be expensive!

Masks: A special facial mask of dry oatmeal and warm water is a home-made treat. Smooth it on, let it dry, then rinse off with warm water. You can practically feel a healthy pink glow coming to your cheeks! Sure, there are zillions of masks available for sale - but, try this one first. You may be surprised. While you're in the kitchen why not save two drained and cooled tea bags to place over weary eye-lids. What a relaxing treat and it only takes five minutes. Don't leave yet - that cucumber in the fridge makes a great refresher. Rub a slice over your skin before moisturizer.

Boosters: If dry skin taunts you even after facials, moisturizers and extra pampering maybe your skin needs to be rejuvenated. Air conditioning, heating and stress rob our skin of precious moisture. Try one of the new moisture "trap" gels or creams. But, don't forget that moisture also must come from within. Drinking 6-8 glasses of water each and every day is a beauty must.

You'll spend the rest of your life taking care of your skin. Every day, every night another cleansing, another regimen for looking your best. It'll get boring - maybe a hassle at times. But remember - you can always let a bad haircut grow out, lose five pounds or try a new lipcolor! Skin that has been abused, misused and unloved for years on end will be there to haunt you. As you peer into the mirror in your early twenties and notice the little crow's feet setting up camp around your eyes you'll wish you hadn't cheated with cleansing or over-indulged in tanning.

Proper skin care will assure you of the beautiful pure "canvas" that you'll need for the next exciting chapter - "The Real-You" Makeover!

Chapter 8
Make-up Accenting the Positive

Making the most of what Mother Nature gave you is what make-up is all about. We all possess beauty assets that have been there all along—a great nose, wide-set eyes, maybe full pouty lips.

Whatever your personal attributes may be, learning how to accent the positive and pay down the negative is our goal for this chapter.

Before we begin let's talk about five rules to help you become your most beautiful self:

Rule 1—Work with what nature gave you whenever possible

Rule 2—Always keep an open mind about changing yourself.

Rule 3—Cultivate your own unique beauty.

Rule 4—Stop trying to look like everyone else and be realistic about your limitations.

Rule 5—Set aside ample time to pamper yourself.

Cosmetics are the "tools" used in the art of makeup. They are intended to enhance and beautify the natural you as well as accentuate features that may otherwise remain unnoticed.

But, as you know, it is the hand that manipulates the tools that is the major factor in determining the end result.

Models and actresses know that the real trick is to look beautiful, not beautifully made up. It takes time and practice, but once the techniques are mastered, no more that eight to twelve minutes are needed to "do your face." Quite frankly, I think it is waste of time to spend an hour putting on makeup.

Your Beauty Kit

Your beauty kit doesn't have to cost a fortune, nor is a duffel bag full of cosmetics necessary or desirable. High quality makeup brushes, tweezers and a nice efficient container for these items are worthwhile investments, for they last a long time. Cleansing lotions, astringents, moisturizers and cosmetic items can often be purchased in economy sizes. A wise makeup shopper, once she knows her proper color scheme, buys cosmetics in a discount store or waits until her particular department store line is running a special or one of those terrific "Gift with Purchase" promotions.

You'll need:

Skin Care Items for your skin type
Foundation
Concealer
Translucent Loose Powder
Compact Powder
Blusher (powder for normal to oily skin, or creme
    for dry skin)
eyeliner pencils
eyeshadows—highlighter or "base color"
    —lid color
    —contour color
Mascara and eyelash comb/eyebrow brush
lipliner
lipcolor
lip gloss
eyebrow makeup

Now don't panic. It only *looks* like a lot of stuff. you don't need to spend six months worth of babysitting money on this. Most important—don't buy anything until you know for sure what colors you'll be needing.

If you need professional help to get it together, many beauty experts are available in you local department stores waiting to give you lots of helpful advice.

Collect all of your "goodies," a towel , a stand-up mirror, and position yourself in strong natural light with all items comfortably within your reach. Follow these easy instructions without interruptions several times within the next week. Before long you'll learn to experiment with color combinations of your own. Ease of application comes from experience and practice.

My Finishing Touches Beauty Plan

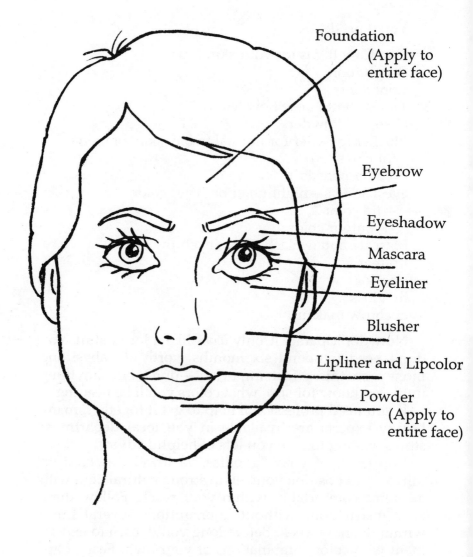

Foundation
(Apply to
entire face)

Eyebrow

Eyeshadow

Mascara

Eyeliner

Blusher

Lipliner and Lipcolor

Powder
(Apply to
entire face)

Foundation

After moisturizer, foundation is the base of all makeup. It hides small flaws and evens poor skin coloring. In addition, it acts as protection from the elements—wind, sun and water. It goes without saying that moisturizer and foundation should be applied to clean skin.

You might not choose to wear foundation every day, and if your skin is in extremely good condition you might not choose to wear it all over.

There are two basic kinds of foundation: liquid and cream. Liquid is lighter and gives less coverage. Cream is heavier and is often used by models and actresses as it insures flawless coverage. Of the two types of foundations there are still many types:

Oil Based—The color is suspended in oil and can look very heavy. Gives excellent coverage. Can clog pores, though.

Water Based—Looks natural and helps moisturize the skin. Excellent for normal to dry skin. Has a tiny amount of oil.

Oil Free—Best for oily skin as it may actually absorb oil from the skin. It contains no oil, and therefore will not clog pores. It must be blended quickly.

Choose the shade that matches your skin tone as closely as possible. Try the color on your clean face in natural daylight . If you can't see where it starts and stops—it is the right color.

Using a cosmetic sponge dot a small amount on your forehead, nose, cheeks and chin. Next, spread the foundation evenly and gently in an upward, outward motion until it is completely blended. Avoid your hairline and eyebrow as dried foundation may discolor and look cakey and dirty. Check your entire face for any lines of demarcation.

Concealer—This optional step is used either before or after foundation to hide blemishes, broken capillaries, lighten dark circles under the eyes or camouflage dark spots.

The easiest ones to use are in stick form and can be blended easily.

If your problem is dark circles do not apply the product directly on the problem area—but just below. Don't try to lighten the area drastically. Don't use white concealer; a shade or two lighter than your foundation is best.

Don't use a concealer if the problem is puffiness. The concealer will only draw undue attention to problem.

"Pat" your concealer on the necessary areas—do not rub, tug or pull, especially the delicate skin around your eyes.

Powder—Powder sets your makeup to help it look better longer, and does away with shine. You'll want to use a loose powder when applying your fresh face of makeup and a compact for touch ups throughout the day.

It's best to work with the no-color translucent powders. Otherwise you may start to look chalky or ashy. A spritz of cool water over your powder will set it beautifully as will alleviate a too-heavy, cakey appearance.

Use a large makeup brush, large clean puff or cotton ball to apply, shaking off any excess product first.

Deep tones skins can look gray if powder is too light. Translucent powder is available in lovely deep shades.

Keep loose powder handy throughout your makeup application. A quick stroke over your blusher (next step) will help it to blend in with the rest of your makeup without and do away with any lines of demarcation.

Blush—Now you have prepared a clean flawless "canvas" on which to create the new you make-over! Natural, flattering colors well bring your face alive!

Who can live without blusher! It makes everyone look better: glowing, alive, and healthy.

Personally, I think blusher is the most misplaced, misused cosmetic of all. Blusher is one of three focal points on your "make-over face." Your eyes and lips are the other two. Each of these areas need to have the same color intensity. If you're wearing pale pink lipcolor, do not wear black eyeliner and dark brown eyeshadow with a pastel pink blusher. I realize that trends and fads come and go with regard to makeup just as with hair and fashion—but I'll not try to teach you fads and trends. You'll pick those up from friends and magazines. I'll teach the "forever basics" that you'll use for a lifetime.

Now, a few tips for application:

Start with a very small amount and build up one layer at a time if you desire a darker coverage. It's much easier to add than to take away.

Constantly blend blusher to alleviate harsh edges.

Use blusher to highlight and contour by applying to temples, under jaw line and tip of nose

Use a creme blusher under a powder blusher of the color for very dry skin or for a more dramatic look.

The rest is practice and proper placement. The first thing I have my students do is look straight into a mirror and suck their cheeks in *hard*. Gently *feel* the bone structure of your face. Study the contours carefully.

Where does the blusher go?

Put blush right where you blush naturally, in the middle of your cheekbones—the "apple" of your cheeks. Additionally, follow these helpful hints to contour your specific face shape:

A *round* face can look slimmer if blusher is blended high on the cheekbone.

A *long*, narrow face will appear slightly wider if blusher is applied at the outer edge of the "apple" and toward the ear.

A *triangular or a heart-shaped face* will look less sharp if blusher is blended high on the cheekbone, out towards the ear and gently swept towards the outer edges of the temples. (Please avoid hairline.)

A *square* face will be softer and more feminine by blusher applied at the lower side of the cheekbone, back and up toward the ear.

A few more "blushing" beauty secrets

* Apply blusher slightly darker if you'll be in any artificial light
* Never bring blusher down too far on your face. It should stop at a point even with the bottom of your nostrils.
* Color brought in too close to your nose will close up your face and can make your nose appear larger.
* Color brought up or in too close to your eyes will make them look small and puffy.
* If you have dark skin, wear a slightly brighter blusher.
* Don't be afraid to accent high, chiseled cheekbones. (Lucky girl!)
* Keep cheek color and lip color in the same color "family." Use a pink lip color with a rose blush, etc.

Eyeliner

Eyeliner is pretty much a matter of changing with the times. Some years it's "in" some years it's out. Some girls look better without liner at all, but those with small light eyes profit greatly from a delicate line that defines. Liner should be as close to the lashes as possible and barely more than a sliver in width is best. Tiny dots of eyeliner pencil smudged together at the base of your lashes will give the illusion of a line, but without the harshness of a drawn line.

If you're using eyeliner you should apply it to both top and bottom lids to create a balanced look.

Never bring the liner all the way into the inside corner of your eye as it will make eyes look smaller.

Eyeshadow

You've kept your powder brush handy so dust lightly across your eyelids to prepare your "canvas."

Deciding where to put the color is the easy part. Deciding which colors to choose and how many can be a little tricky.

Use my Eye Shadow Selection Chart when in doubt:

EYE COLOR	SHADOW COLOR	RESULTS
Deep Brown	Plum Deep Teal Copper Rich Pink	Add sparkle to eye area; makes whites of eyes look whiter
Blue	Plum Brown Pink Beige	Good accent color Intensifies blue Makes eyes seem clearer, brighter Brings out grey tones
Green or Hazel	Charcoal Gray Pink True Blue Brown Green	Brings out the green Highlights green eyes Makes green clearer Brings out gold or brown highlights
Brown	Plum Sage Blue-Gray Lavender	All will tend to enrich the warmth and depth of brown eyes through contrast

1. Round

2. Almond

3. Drooping

4. Deep-set

1. **To make eyes look deeper set**—Place deeper coloring in eyelid crease. Avoid pale frosted shades.

2. **To make eyes look more prominent**—Concentrate color on the eye bone; use a light or frosted shade on your eyelid.

3. **To make eyes look farther apart**—Sweep a darker color up and out from the center to the outer corners of lid.

4. **To make eyes look larger**—Sweep color out to the side, along browbone and under lower lid.

5. **To make eyes look more open**—Place shadow along the lid with lots of color in the crease. "Cheat" a little color just above the crease also.

Honestly—I could go on for pages and pages *just* about eyeshadow. It's fun to experiment and the possibilities are endless.

Just remember that the colors you choose and the way in which you apply eye shadow are pretty much a matter of personal taste and current fashion. Ordinarily, discreet colors look best for daytime. Think of browns, grays and dusty versions of the jewel tones, (violets, fuchsias, bright blues, topaz, emerald). For special occasions or evening more brilliant colors are acceptable.

Eyes that look "drawn on" are not attractive. It's this kind of heavy eye makeup application that will make your parents a *little* upset i.e.,"You're not going out of this house with that black junk around your eyes!"

Stick with eyeshadow colors which compliment the natural eye color rather than make an overly obvious fashion statement.

You'll have a set of gorgeous peepers and a much happier set of parents!

Curling Lashes

Curling lashes before applying mascara opens up the eye. When the white of the eyes isn't shadowed by overhanging lashes, it looks clearer, whiter and brighter. If you wear glasses, curling is a must to keep lashes from sweeping the lenses.

It causes absolutely no harm to the lashes when done gently and correctly. Grip the lashes in the curler and hold. Take care to not grip too close to the root as to pinch the eyelid. (Ouch! I did that the very first time.) Count to twenty. Don't squeeze the curler too firmly; you'll get crimped rather than softly upturned lashes, and if you are rough you can damage the hairs.

Mascara

When properly utilized, mascara can be one of the most effective cosmetics in your beauty kit—too many of us just flick our lashes through a mascara brush and call it a day. But that's hardly a good beginning.

Follow my model's tips for lush beautiful lashes:

* Automatic mascara with its bristly little wand brush is the easiest to use.

* "Layer" your mascara in thin, even coats

* Do the top side of your upper lashes first.

* Clumping of lashes is caused by rushing mascara application. Go slowly, and separate lashes with a brush if necessary. Using the tip of the wand eliminates clumping.

* Look down into a mirror to do your top lashes. You'll alleviate "speckles" on your brow bone.

* Look straight into a mirror for bottom lashes. Apply mascara with the brush held vertically. You'll discover lashes you never knew you had!

* For extra lushness, let your mascara dry for a minute. Then dust a little face powder over your lashes and apply a second coat of mascara. You'll love the extra length and fullness.

Eyebrows

Eyebrows are the "frames" of the eye. Never alter the natural arch of the brow and never tweeze the top side of the brow. (Notice that I said tweeze—not pluck. You pluck chickens!)

It is best to tweeze immediately after a facial, shower or bath when the pores are open. Hairs will come out easier.

Follow these tips. Be patient. The first time is definitely the worst.

Brows should not extend beyond a point directly above the inner corner of eye, arching over eye's center and ending at a line formed by placing a pencil from your nose to the outer corner of your eye.

* Tweeze only one hair at a time.
* Never shave your eyebrows. The hair will grow back stubby.
* Tweeze only in the direction that hair grows.
* After tweezing, it's wise to apply an antiseptic or witch hazel, avoiding the chance of infection.
* Examine brows in bright natural light to spot any stragglers.

Now that you've refined your brow to a clean line, it's time to think about eyebrow makeup. Most people think in terms of darkening, but models learn early that brows need lightening in most cases. Heavy brows tend to give the impression of a frown. Lightening can be done temporarily with a dusting of baby powder or with one of the brow-lightening makeups on the market. When brows are very dark, consider having them bleached professionally. Don't attempt this at home. Blondes should never use black to darken brows. It's too harsh even for most brunettes. Use a brown, gray, beige or taupe pencil according to your hair coloring. Make light feathery strokes rather than solid lines at all times.

As a final touch, brush eyebrows in an upward motion with your eyebrow brush. You'll remove any loose makeup particles as well as open up the eye area even more.

Lips

The third facial focal point is your lipcolor. Once you've mastered the use of a lip pencil and a lipstick brush you'll wonder how you managed before.

You can have all of your makeup applied *except* lipcolor and still look pale and washed-out. Lipcolor activates our entire face. Remember to stay in the same color "family" that you selected for your blusher and nail color.

If your mouth is too large, too full, too thin, or uneven, these problems can be corrected by knowledgeable application of liplines. This lipliner should match or blend in with your lipcolor.

Thin lips—Cover outline of your lips with foundation. Draw new lipline with pencil, slightly outside your natural lip line. Fill in with color.

Full Lips—Cover outline of your lips with foundation. Pencil new outline slightly inside natural lip line. The key word here is *slightly*. Fill in color.

Un-Even Lips—Cover outline of your lips with foundation. Pencil in a new outline so that the uneven lip will match its mate. Fill in with color.

To Make Pouty Lips—Use a darker lip color to fill in the lower lip, a lighter one on the upper lip. Keep the difference in the shades very subtle—just a little lighter or darker. Top it off with a clear gloss.

Tips for Lips

* Invest in a good sable lipstick brush. Practice starting with the little "cupid's bow" in the center of your top lip. Now, paint around the little "peaks." On your lower lip, center the fullest part under the tip of your nose.

* Put lip pencils in the freezer for a few minutes before sharpening.

* Your teeth will appear whiter and brighter in seconds if you stay away from lipcolor with tones of blue. What shade should you choose? Any orange, orange-red, coral, or clear pink.

105

* If mouth is too small, avoid dark-toned deep red lipcolors which will accentuate its diminutive size.

* Relieve chapped, cracked lips with petroleum jelly, cocoa butter or baby oil, and avoid licking or wetting lips until they heal.

* Set lipcolor to last all day by pressing an ice cube to your freshly made-up mouth. Keeps lipstick from smearing, blurring or creeping into mouth lines.

* If your bathroom make-up mirror has fluorescent light, be sure to check your lipcolor in natural or daylight. Fluorescent light changes the color of all makeup, and it creates some really strange effects on lipcolor and blush.

Selecting Your Best Colors

Now that you know *where* each component of your makeover goes, let's discuss some color combinations to help you always look your best.

BLACK SKIN
Foundation—Skin tones vary from light to very dark. Foundation must be matched to perfection.

Eyes—Black, green, or plum liners, Apricot, purple, russet, or jewel-toned shadows.

Cheeks—Rich honey-bronze, red-based brick, fresh plum.

Lips—Garnet, plum, raisin. Deep vivid colors work best.

FAIR AND FRECKLED
Foundation—Peachy-ivory tones will look natural. Individual is usually fair and has red or auburn hair. This coloring has orange and yellow undertones. Makeup shades should be warm.

Eyes—Medium brown, slate blue, russet, cinnamon, pumpkin, or any other gold-based shadows. Gray or brown eye-liner are good basics. Green would be fun for special occasions. Black would always be too harsh for you.

Cheeks—Apricot or golden peach tones are your best compliment.

Lips—Corals, peachy-beige, and other yellow-based colors such as cinnamon. Where you can stay neutral, rather than bright.

OLIVE
Foundation—This skin tone's most common trait is a green undertone. Warm shades of beige or light tan are best.

Eyes—Black eyeliner is best, but do not apply with a heavy hand. Gray, taupe, or teal shadows are best.

Cheeks—Avoid blushes with blue undertones. Stay with red-based shades such as brick, wine. Amber is also a good choice.

Lips—Avoid orange shades. True reds and clear, rich corals are good.

MEDIUM
Foundation—Yellow-based beige shades look best. If your skin has pink/red undertones stay away from red-based colors.

Eyes—Gray-black or rich-brown eyeliner is best. Shadow picks include: sage, celery, nutmeg, copper, beige, and amber.

Cheeks—Amber peach, coral shades are best.

Lips—Raisin, bronze, mauve.

IVORY
Foundation—Skin is white, almost translucent with bluish undertones. Base should be ivory with a hint of peach or rose. Avoid anything with a yellow undertone.

Eyes—Eyeliner should be gray or golden brown. Navy or teal can be fun for special days. Best shadow picks are rose, blue-gray, pinky-corals, plum and teal. Brown should be soft shades only.

Cheeks—Rose, pink, or coral.

Lips—Steer clear of reds or roses with too much of a blue undertone. Clear pinks, rose, coral, or berry are a good compliment.

A Final Word On Make-Up

The decision to wear make-up is one that you will need to discuss with your parents. This decision is a very personal one. I feel it's most important for you to realize that your clothes, how you wear your hair, how healthy you are, and how much makeup you wear, all makes a statement about who you are as a person. People will look at you and get a certain impression or feeling about you. Make sure it's a feeling you're happy with as well as one that puts out a "message" you're comfortable with.

Chapter 9
Crowning Glory

When a girl's hair looks good, she feels happy about herself, energetic, and pretty no matter what she is wearing. Healthy, beautiful hair is a girl's most treasured natural asset. Of all beauty attributes, hair is the most noticeable—a perfect frame for a lovely face. Hair styling allows you such versatility and variety. A hairdo can make you look taller, younger, older, fresher; bring out your prettiest features and minimize those which are less attractive. You can transform your hair from curly to straight and from straight to curly. To make the most of your own beautiful locks, you must take proper care of your hair and scalp.

The nicest thing you can do for your hair is keep it clean. Once a week may be enough for your hair and scalp, or you may need to shampoo daily. The key is to do what's right for you. When your hair begins to "separate" at the roots and look heavy or oily. It's time for a shampoo. Other girls can tell that their hair is dirty because it hangs limp and flat to their head. You'll know when it's time. Not everyone's hair puts out such an easy "signal," as looking oily when it gets dirty. So let's talk about different types of hair and how to care for them properly.

OILY HAIR

Looks Like:
—Separates and sometimes look darker at roots (especially on light hair).
—Feels heavy and looks limp when dirty.
What to do:
—Never wash your hair in hot water, always warm; then rinse in cool water to close pores in scalp. Hair will be shinier and cleaner!
—Lather two or three times if needed
—Use a shampoo for oily hair
—Use conditioner or creme rinse from your ear level down only

Special Help:
—If your hair is long, learn how to wear it up in french braids or clever off-the-neck hairstyles, especially in warm weather.
—Make sure ends are trimmed every 6-8 weeks.

DRY HAIR

Looks Like:
—Usually has split ends
—Not very shiny
—If it's damaged, it can look like straw
—Can look "bushy" if it's thick
What To Do:
—Use a shampoo for dry or damaged hair
—Use a creme rinse for tangles
—Avoid over-exposure to sun, wind and blow dryers

Special Help:
—"Extra help" conditioner twice a month
—Trim split ends every 6-8 weeks

FLAT HAIR

Looks Like:
—Thin, limp
—Fly-away "look"
—"baby-fine"
What to do:
—Shampoo with gentle PH balanced product
—Use protein conditioner
—Keep ends evenly trimmed; the blunter the cut, the thicker the hair will look
Special Help:
—Stay away from creme rinses that soften and flatten hair
—Keep hair above shoulder length
—Lean over with head upside down if blow drying;

this makes hair appear fuller. A little hair spray for special occasions helps
—Consider a "body perm" for fullness and shape

COARSE, CURLY OR BLACK HAIR

Looks like:
—Thick and wiry
—Curly
—Unruly and out of control
—Often appears dry and bushy
What To Do:
—Shampoo once or twice a week
—Avoid dampness and humidity that causes the "frizzies"
—Keep hair trimmed and thinned to remove excess bulk
Special Help:
—Avoid heat appliances such as blow dryers, hot rollers, and curling irons
—Have hair cut into a "wash and go" style
—Do not attempt straightening kits for extremely curly or black hair at home; have this professionally done
—Avoid allowing hair to become too long and out of control
—Master the excitement and fun of braids and hair ornaments

NORMAL HAIR

Looks Like:
—Shiny and healthy
—Bouncy
—Not too oily, not too dry
What To Do:
—Shampoo when needed
—Creme rinse for tangles and deep conditioner as needed

112

—Rinse well, using cool water
—Trim every 6-8 weeks as needed
Special Help:
—Just because your hair is "normal" now, don't get lazy and over-expose to heat appliances and sunlight

Some Hair Care Do's And Don'ts:

DO

Use a wide tooth plastic comb for de-tangling wet hair
Drink plenty of milk and water to keep hair shiny and bouncy
Remove barrette, pins and other ornaments when sleeping
Use products that are right for you—not just the ones your friends use
Use a fresh, clean towel to dry your hair
Wear a hairstyle that fits your lifestyle
Avoid exposing your hair to excessive sunlight
Wash brushes and combs every two weeks

DON'T

Brush hair when wet; it stretches and breaks
Eat junk food and not expect the ill-effects to show up in your hair
Use real rubber bands in hair; *do* use only coated type
Use handfuls of shampoo; a fifty cent piece sized "dollop" is plenty
Use crimpers and wavers every day
Wear a hairstyle that's not right for you, even if you love it
Comb hair at mealtime
Ever cut your own hair or a friend's; same goes for perms, relaxers, etc.
Look through your favorite magazines or catalogs for a new hairstyle you'd like to try. Now, answer the following questions about the style you selected:

—Does the person in the picture have the same color hair as me?

—Does the person have the same type of hair? Curly, straight, or limp?

—Does the style require more time than you are willing to give before leaving for school?

Sometimes we see pretty pictures of models or actresses in magazines or catalogs and wish we could look like them. Remember that the beautiful redhead's curly bob will not look the same on the sweet, pale blond with stick straight locks!

We have a saying for this—"The grass is always greener on the other side of the fence." It's the truth! I've rarely met a teen with naturally curly hair who didn't at some point wish it were poker straight and vice-versa.

Learn to work with what you've got. An experienced stylist can be honest and realistic when helping you pick out a style. Teens take care of their hair differently now than just a few years ago. Many hairstyles require sprays, spritzes, gels, mousses, and an assortment of clips and appliances. Gone are the days when anyone younger than you mom simply wore her hair in a traditional pony tail or braids! But remember, keep it simple. Too many "extras" can sometimes take away from your healthy "crowning glory"- and that wonderful face of yours.

Special Hair Helpers

Your kitchen can provide a wealth of beauty potions! Try some of nature's best kept beauty secrets, and save yourself a lot of money, as well. Fancy packaging and advertising is not always the best route to follow.

Chamomile Rinse

Brew a chamomile teabag in three cups of boiling water. Let cool and pour through wet hair several times. Adds a natural glow to blonde, light brown, or red hair.

Vegetable Oil Conditioners

Before shampooing, apply a vegetable oil (olive, castor,

corn, or even wheatgerm) to dry ends and up to ear level. Wrap your head in a warm damp towel for about half an hour. Shampoo and rinse well. Hair will be shinier, thicker looking without a residue.

Vinegar Rinse

This rinse is for any type of hair, but works best for brunettes. Mix four cups of water with one-half cup apple cider vinegar as your hair's final rinse after shampooing. It will remove all traces of shampoo and tighten the hair's cuticle, therefore making it appear shinier. It can also restore hair to its natural acidity.

Lemon Rinse

This natural highlighting rinse is perfect for blondes and light brunettes. Add the juice of one fresh lemon with two cups of cold water and use as your final shampoo rinse. Please be advised that your hair will lighten (and dry out) if exposed to sunlight while the lemon juice remains on.

Rosemary Rinse

To reduce dandruff, check excessive oiliness and bring sparkle to black or dark brown hair, brew a handful of dried rosemary in two cups of boiling water. Let cool and strain. Use as your final shampoo rinse.

Egg Shampoo

This formula has been handed down to us by our great-grandmothers. Separate two eggs and whip the whites until peaks are formed. Add a tablespoon of water to the egg yolks and blend until the mixture is creamy. Combine the beaten whites with the yolks and apply half of the mixture to your damp hair. Wait five minutes, rinse hair with cool water (not hot—you don't want an omelet!) Use the second half of the mixture and rinse thoroughly. Towel dry your hair and style as usual.

Shapes And Styles

You've learned what "recipe" to follow for your own hair type. Now, let's decide which hairstyles will best compliment the shape of your face.

But, if you're like most girls, you may have a difficult time determining what shape *you're* in. First, pull your hair back of your face. Look straight into a mirror and trace the outline of your face onto the glass with the edge of a piece of soap. Take a step back and study the shape. Is it an oval? How about a square?

Follow my illustrations as guidelines to help you select your best "do."

#1 OVAL FACE

The lucky lass with an oval-shaped face can wear practically any style as long as it is appropriate for her hair type.

#2 ROUND FACE

GOOD	NOT SO GOOD
—simple	—round, poofy
—shoulder length	—hair cluttering neckline
—smooth	—flatness on top
—fullness on top	

#3 HEART FACE

GOOD	NOT SO GOOD
—fullness at chin	—fullness at temples and
—widow's peak exposed	cheekbones
—soft bangs	—heavy bangs
	—hair tucked behind ears

#4 SQUARE FACE

GOOD	NOT SO GOOD
—founded styles	—fullness at chin
—softness	—flatness on top
—no clutter around chin-line	

#5 OBLONG FACE

GOOD	NOT SO GOOD
—soft bangs	—center part
—chin length	—long and straight
—soft curls	—exposed ears

Whatever length or style you prefer, have your hair professionally cut or trimmed. The basis of all good-looking, long-lasting hairstyles is a super cut. The frequency of salon visits depends mainly on the length of your hair and only partially on its style. Short styles require more frequent care and may need to be trimmed every three to four weeks. A medium length style can hold its shape up to six weeks, while long hair may need only to be trimmed one-half inch or so every 8-10 weeks.

Establishing a trusting relationship with your stylist is crucial. Don't flip-flop back and forth between salons. You'll never establish any real loyalty or consistency by going to a different stylist each month or so.

Some Care And Styling Terms To Make Your Selection Easier

Blunt Cut—Hair is all one length straight cuts that are leveled, encouraging the ends to turn under. Blonde hair that is blunt cut will often appear shinier, as light is reflected off it more effectively. This cutting technique is wonderful for making fine, thin, soft hair appear thicker.

Layered Cut—Hair is cut at a succession of different lengths. This cut is particularly nice for short wavy or curly hair as it will encourage more curl!

Tapered Cut—Either scissors or a razor is used to cut across the hair at an angle. A good example of a tapered cut being used is to angle from your forehead down to the end of a blunt cut in order to frame the face attractively.

Temporary Hair Color—A rinse that washes out with each shampoo.

Semi-Permanent Hair Color—Gives a color change that lasts about one month. These coat and slightly penetrate the hair shaft.

Permanent Hair Color—Actually alters the hair structure. It cannot be washed out and will stay on the hair as it grows.

(Please note: The haircolor given to you by Mother

Nature is most often your best choice. Artificial coloring of your hair is a decision that should be discussed with an adult and with your stylist. It should never be done by you or by a friend, "just for fun.")

Relaxer—A chemical process that takes the excessive curliness or frizziness out of black hair. Be sure that your hair is strong and healthy before using this or any chemical process.

Permanent Or "Perm"—A perm will alter the structure of your hair to conform to the shape of the curler or "perm rod" that is used. The effect can be slightly wavy to tight spiral curls, depending on the size of the rod. It will last from two to six months, depending on the length of your hair and how quickly it grows.

Conditioner—Applied after shampooing, it coats the hair shaft and acts as a buffer against external conditions. It helps bring back life and luster to mistreated hair, adds shine to dry hair, and helps tame fly-away hair.

Creme Rinse—Not to be confused with a conditioner; its basic purpose is to de-tangle yours locks. It has no therapeutic value.

How To Shampoo

1. Brush your hair to distribute oil and loosen dead cells from the scalp.

2. Use warm water. Wet hair thoroughly. Throw your head back so the soil rinses out of your hair and runs off behind you, not down your face.

3. Pour a small amount of shampoo into your palm. Rub your hands together to work up a lather, then work through your hair with your fingers. Work suds from your scalp to the ends of your hair and massage gently.

4. Rinse thoroughly in warm water, then cool.

5. You do not need to lather a second time unless hair is very dirty or oily.

6. Use an instant conditioner or creme rinse right after rinsing shampoo out of your hair to de-tangle and add shine.

7. Gently towel dry.

8. Style.

How To Blow-Dry Beautifully

It never fails. I go to my stylist and leave the salon thinking I can duplicate her blow-drying magic the next time I wash my hair. Have you ever noticed how easy it looks when they do it? Well—I coerced my stylist into sharing a few hints:

1. Your hair should be damp-not wet before you begin.

2. Start drying at a higher setting, but switch to a lower setting after two minutes.

3. Always hold the blow dryer at least six inches from your hair and keep the dryer in motion at all times.

4. Styling as you dry is possible with a round brush with heat-resistant bristles. Be sure your hair is almost dry before you start styling with the brush. The results will be more natural than if you had used rollers or a curling iron.

5. Comb your hair into sections as you begin to dry. Use a wide-toothed comb and part the hair into the following sections: sides, sides front, sides back, back, and top front. Dry one section at a time. Do the sides first and the top front last.

6. For more volume, divide your hair into smaller sections or flip your head forward so that your hair hangs down while you blow-dry.

7. For smooth straight hair, use the round brush to grab the ends of your hair; then pull the brush downward. So the hair is held taut. Bring the dryer across the top of your hair. Now brush the hair downward with long, smooth strokes. Work slowly all around your head, section by section.

8. To turn your hair under, use the round brush to twirl the hair from underneath. Roll the brush down and under. Aim the blow-dryer under the brush. To have your ends flip up, do just the opposite.

9. If your hair is curly or wavy, you may wish to use a

diffuser or heat lamp to dry your hair without straightening the curves.

A final tip for blow-drying—don't do it every day. Excessive heat is not good for hair.

Have fun as you experiment with new hairstyles. Wearing your hair the same way each day can really put you in a rut. You can find some variation in simple changes such as pulling your hair back with a great barrette, parting your hair a difficult way, or rolling it instead of wearing it straight.

Whenever I've been tempted to do something drastic to my hair (that I'll later regret) it's usually because I've been wearing it the same way day after day. Most changes that are truly impulsive are quite regrettable.

Finally, the perfect treat for you or a friend is a *scalp massage*. A massage stimulates circulation in the scalp and can even stimulate hair growth beneath your scalp. Massaging activates the tiny oil glands at the base of each hair follicle and loosens the scalp for greater elasticity and bounce.

1. Place both thumbs against the base of neck and stretch your other fingers out with the cushions of each fingertip against your scalp.

2. Making sure that your scalp is moving and not just your fingers, rotate your hands gently on your scalp for 3-5 minutes.

3. Continue massaging scalp directing attention to your temples, top of scalp and all around until you reach your hairline.

A scalp massage is the ultimate pamper session. You owe yourself some "T.L.C." once in awhile.

If you're like most teens you'll experiment and try lots of different hairstyles until you find the perfect one for you. Don't be afraid to try new things in order to find your true "crowning glory."

Chapter 10
Fingers and Toes

I noticed my husband's perfectly manicured finger-nails before I noticed anything else about him. Sound strange? Maybe. However, I have observed over the years some interesting things about good grooming habits and the individuals they belong to.

Well manicured nails typically belong to a person who is meticulous about everything they do. Their closets, desks, and dresser drawers are probably quite orderly too.

Likewise, chipped, half-polished, ragged nails usually go along with a somewhat "haphazard" approach to grooming.

When I booked models I always noticed the little things—nails, shoes, purses. Were they neat and clean or just good enough to slide by?

A complete manicure should be part of your body pampering at least once a week. Your hands speak for you, so let them say the nicest things—always.

Let's get started.—The special routine used for keeping your fingernails in tip-top shape is called a *manicure*.

You will need the following items:

1. Clear polish	8. Liquid soap
2. Color of Polish	9. Nail clippers
3. Cotton balls	10. Nail polish remover
4. Cuticle remover	11. Orange stick
5. Emery board	12. Paper towel
6. Fingernail brush	13. Small bowl
7. Hand lotion	14. Small hand towel

Spread these items out on a towel to protect table tops and counters.

Beauty Routine for Ten Perfect Nails

1. Remove old polish.

2. File dry nails with smooth side of emery board to oval shape. Never file wet nails. Make certain that nails are not too pointed or squared and that they are kept fairly short.

3. Soak fingers (up to first knuckle) in warm, soapy water. Better yet, take a bubble bath, and let the bath water work wonders on any hardened cuticles. *Cuticles* are the tough or hard skin that grows up around the area where your nail grows and your skin leaves off. It doesn't really do any harm except to be just as tempting for nervous chewing as your fingernails can sometimes be! It also makes your nails appear shorter.

4. Gently push back dampened cuticle with the blunt end of your orange stick. No, the stick is not orange in color but made from the wood of an orange tree. It does not easily splinter and is very soft, making it perfect for working near the delicate skin surrounding your nails. "Hang nails" are the ragged little pieces of skin that mysteriously appear just below your fingernails practically overnight! Do not bite them as they can be *very* painful. If one of these painful little skin tabs pops up on you, clip it carefully with your nail clippers soaked in alcohol, and then apply a drop of antiseptic.

5. For stubborn cuticle areas, go back and use cuticle remover.

6. Gently scrub nails with nail brush and check for any stubborn dirt with slanted end of orange stick.

7. Dry nails with towel.

8. Resting your hand on a clean paper towel, brush on one clear coat of nail polish. Make it very thin and even taking care not to allow polish to touch your skin. If it does, simply wrap a little cotton around the end of your orange stick, dip in polish remover and use as a cotton swab to remove boo-boos.

9. Let nails dry at least 10 minutes before applying hand lotion.

10. For girls who are using a neutral or brighter polish,

you would apply two coats of color after the clear polish as it now serves as a base coat. When color has dried for 15-20 minutes, apply another coat of clear as a top coat to protect. A little extra clear polish on underside of nail tip keeps color from wearing off as quickly.

There you have it -—a beautiful set of fingernails to be proud of! Treat yourself to a lotion massage when nails are completely dry. Start at elbows and end at fingernails. As well groomed as they are now, even the most dedicated nail biter would have second thoughts!

Let's point our beautiful fingers at a few last **Do's** and **Don'ts**.

DO	DON'T
Rub hand lotion onto cuticle area before going to bed	Wear dark or bright nail colors for school, especially active days. Chips on dark polish look yuc!
Apply only thin coats of polish	Wear decals, charms or glitter. (to be honest, do they ever look appropriate?)
Allow nails to dry before going to bed	
Use hair dryer to dry nails fast, but no closer than 12 inches	Bite your nails! It doesn't just look bad, but you'll swallow germs
Place cotton balls between your toes before polishing	Use metal nail files
	Allow polish to chip halfway off before removing for good
Wear shoes that fit properly to avoid painful foot conditions	Use your nails as a "tool"—they will break
	Allow several different lengths of nails if they begin to break

Mending a Nail

There's nothing more frustrating than breaking just one or two nails out of a perfect ten! You can't bear the thought of cutting all of them yet the two "stubs" you're left with ruin everything. What's a girl to do? There's hope!

You can keep a special ready made nail-repair kit on hand, or you can mend your nail with the tools you have at home. You can use the little tissues that come in on eyeglass cleaner kit. You can also use handkerchief linen.

Tear off just a small piece of linen or paper just slightly larger than the split, chip or break. Wrap it around the "boo-boo" so that the ends can tuck under the nail. Brush the patch with "sooper dooper" clear glue. Using your orange stick remove all the bumps or wrinkles. A small amount of polish remover on the tip on your orange stick will make this easier. When the patch is completely dry, apply a base coat followed by two coats of polish and a top coat.

You'll hardly be able to see the patch. I've had patch jobs last until my nail grew back out.

False Nails

When I first started modelling the only alternative to a broken nail was a patch or plastic false nails that were glued on top of your own. Although they are pre-shaped they always needed more customizing, and I never seemed to apply them properly or keep them on once I did.

Acrylic or "Solar" or liquid nails can be a wonderful alternative. When there is no nail length for the manicurist to work with, an aluminum or cardboard base is wrapped around the nail first. Then powder and liquid ingredients are mixed together to form a milky looking substance which is applied, dried and shaped over the form to become a new nail. The form is removed, the new nail is filed, shaped and buffed and can then be polished to look like your own.

I do not suggest you try this at home. I did once and had disastrous results. Some things are better left to the pros, and this is one.

Whether you are repairing one nail (substance is simply applied on top like a patch) or obtaining ten new beautiful nails, let's talk about the pros and cons to this procedure.

PRO	CONS
Nails look beautiful, long and well groomed	Regular maintenance of fill-ins required as nails grow
Alleviates finding time at home for a manicure	Can become inconvenient and costly
Going for fill-ins and manicure make you feel pampered	A fungus can grow between your own nail and the artificial nail substance. (New substances on the market are more porous. Ask questions!)
Nails are always uniformly shaped	Have to be careful what other kinds of products your nails come in contact with.

Some of us just have a miserable time growing and maintaining lovely nails. If you are one of those people, maybe artificial nails are for you—but remember, it is a commitment.

Quick Reminders for Hand and Nail Care

* Rub lotion or creme on the cuticle area before going to bed.
* Apply polish in thin, even coats.
* Wear rubber gloves when doing household chores.
* Give your hands a massage with petroleum jelly before going to bed and wear white cotton gloves or special nail mitts to trap the moisture while you sleep. Your hands will be their most beautiful ever!
* Do not use your nails as a tool. Dial the phone with the eraser end of a pencil, etc.
* A cut lemon can remove stains such as ink and food dyes. Polish remover also works for stubborn stains. Remember to rinse hands immediately in cool water and apply lotion to prevent dry skin.
* Don't wear dark or bright polish for school or active

days. Chips and worn-off ends will look un-tidy. Choose clear or neutrals

* Don't be a nail biter. It doesn't just look bad—it's bad for you.

* Use a **moist pumice stone** to rub away calluses at sides of nails and rough spots on feet, too.

* Eat lots of protein-rich foods such as eggs, meats, cheese and milk for strong nails—but be careful not to overload the cholesterol!

* Emery boards should never be used on wet nails

* Metal fingernail files are too brutal—emery boards or buffing boards only.

* Short, weak, unhealthy nails should be filed square for strength until they can grow into a pretty oval.

* The darker the polish, the shorter your nails will appear.

A Treat For Your Feet

Nothing will make you feel more pampered than a *pedicure*. Pretty feet are the perfect finishing touch. Models know that their feet must be as perfect as their hands. You will feel *so* "together." During the warm months you can wear your nifty sandals with pride. Basically, a pedicure is the same as a manicure. Here are some additional helpful hints.

* Always clip toenails straight across to avoid ingrown toenails.

* Use the coarse side of the emery board if your big toe has a thickened nail.

* Tuck cotton or tissue between your toes before polishing.

* Smooth calluses and rough heels with a dampened pumice stone. (available at the drug store)

* Apply lots of lotion after nails are dry.

* Wear shoes that fit properly (leather is best to allow your skin to "breathe")

* Elevate your feet when you get home after a busy day.

* Your feet tend to be larger at the end of the day—keep this in mind if you shop for shoes at night.

* Sprinkle foot powder or baby powder in your shoes for a fresh treat.

Follow these tips and remember to allow yourself special time to indulge in the treat of a manicure and pedicure.

Note—a wonderful gift for mom would be a "gift certificate" from you for a nail pampering session!

Chapter 11
What To Wear, When, Why, and How

T rends can't be taught.
Style is acquired.
Taste is something you're born with.
When it comes right down to it, fashion is nothing—
style is everything and style is class.

The human race started covering their bodies with
clothing to be modest, protect their bodies from the elements and for decoration or adornment. Eventually,
adornment took precedence over practicality. As a result
of pressure from peer groups, economics and changes in
our lifestyles, the fashion industry is now one of the
largest industries in the world.

We start out wanting to look like everyone else. The
right tennis shoes, the right sweater worn the right way.
As children we feel safer dressing in a communal way.
You know, safety in numbers. Most of us stay in this mode
until our adolescent years when acceptances is so important—and usually harder than ever before. Then for many
girls an air of individuality evolves, enabling the true
personality to really shine through. For many parents—
this is the period they've dreaded since the day their
daughters were out of diapers. For many parents, this
period of inner development (and outer!) can manifest
itself with kooky hair styles, interesting make-up technique and the trendiest of the trendy in apparel. While I do
not believe that your personality should be stifled while
you're growing and establishing your own sense of
"self"; I do feel that each of us needs to know what is
appropriate for each and every situation.

"Doing your own thing" is fine—but being strange just
for the sake of being different, or for shock value is not. I
once had a girl in class who would wear inappropriate
clothing just to get a reaction. Well, she got a reaction all
right. The other students shunned her because they were
confused as to what message she was trying to convey.
Was she purposely trying to not fit in or did she genuinely
think she was attractive?

It is much easier to dress to please yourself than to please others. What may look great on your best friend may not look so great on you. But, the temptation is always there to mimic someone's look—especially that of someone you admire.

Taking a Fashion "Inventory"

This will probably be your mom's favorite part of the book—organize your closet and dresser drawers! It's not as bad as it sounds; it can actually be sort of fun.

Let's begin by taking everything out of your closet and piling it on the floor (clean floor, of course). Start by making neat piles on your bed of things that are the same; pants together, blouses together, and so on. Then, hang them in your closet the same way. Don't "double up" clothes on one hanger because you'll have such a hard time finding that favorite shirt when you're running late for school! If you're really clever, try hanging each category by color as well.

Now it's time for dresser drawers. (The very thought may frighten some of you.) I'll tell you from experience that you'll be better off dumping them (one at a time, please) on your bed and go from there. You should have one sock drawer, one underwear drawer and so on. If you have just a small amount of one particular thing, you can use one drawer. Maybe hair barrettes and hose can share a space.

Helpful hint—Cut shoe boxes so that they are one-half inch shorter than the top of your drawers, arrange inside and use to keep things from running together. For items that need more room, use empty gift boxes in different sizes. Some of my students have covered them in pretty paper so that they have something nice to look at each time they open the drawer.

We've saved the most fun for last—closet shelves and floor! If the shelves in your closet are too high for you to reach, make sure that you don't put anything up there that you have to reach very often. Shelves are a good place for out of season purses and shoes, books (certainly not this one), extra boxes and various uncompleted projects. Clear, plastic shoe boxes, or regular boxes well labeled on the end are super for closet top spruce up.

Do you throw shoes, dirty clothes and assorted other goodies in the bottom of your closet at night? Shame on you if you do, as you'll just make life so much harder if you ever need to find anything, and of course, *some day* you will. The plastic, see- through boxes are great here, too, as are any types of boxes, crates and especially stacking vegetable bins in pretty plastics. This is a terrific rainy day project, and to do it properly, it will take just about all day.

One of the hardest parts of cleaning out closets and dresser drawers is gaining the ability to get rid of things we no longer need or have use for.How about the orange lace dress Aunt Lilly gave you two Christmases ago? Get the picture? We have all had things we kept for sentimental (or family) reasons. That's fine. It's important to hold on to special things that have special meaning for us, but those items don't need to take up valuable space in what may be an already crowded closet or drawer.

Keep those treasured items in a chest or trunk for safekeeping. (Close enough, of course, so that you can pull out the orange dress if Aunt Lilly should visit!)

Do you have a hamper for your dirty clothes? If so, please see to it that they make it to the hamper and not under your bed or in the closet. Ask Mother where she would like you to put clothing that is in need of repair. You may be able to sew on a missing button, but you'll probably want her to handle any major repair.

You see, having a place for everything and everything in its place will make you feel so good!

By starting out with an organized, pretty area for your clothes to "live", you'll find that it's so much easier to (1) put together lots of great outfits because you'll spot your garments at a moments glance and (2) keep what you have neater and in better shape.

Mom will be tickled pink, and you just may never have to miss the bus again!

Establishing Your Fashion Personality

What's that? Well it's the real you shining through. Fashion is an extension of our personality. Is there anything hanging in your closet that you've never felt good in? It's probably because it's just not "you."

Who are "you?" Let's see. Take this little quiz first and then we'll determine your fashion personality.

1. When I grow up I'd rather:
   A. get married and have babies.
   B. move to the mountains and make pottery.
   C. fly off to Paris or New York and try acting.
   D. enter the hustle-bustle of the corporate world.

2. My favorite subject in school is:
   A. physical education
   B. English literature
   C. government and social studies
   D. math and computer science

3. In the afternoon following school I enjoy:
   A. playing tennis or bike riding
   B. meeting at a friends house to talk and "dream"
   C. writing poetry
   D. getting a "head start" on my homework

4. If I could live anywhere it would be:
   A. on a ranch raising horses.
   B. in a flat in Greenwich Village.
   C. in an antique filled mansion on the French Riviera.
   D. in a condominium complex of young professionals.

If you selected all "A" answers you are **"All Natural."** You love the great outdoors and love the simplicity of a great pair of jeans with one terrific tweed blazer. You've never been one to plan your wardrobe around the latest fashion magazine. Your hairstyle is low maintenance and your make-up very natural. You're ecology minded, careful about what you eat and probably in good physical condition.

If you have mostly "B" answers, you are a "**trendy.**" Only the latest, most excited and highly avant garde for this exciting girl. You are always interesting to visit with because you keep up with all the newest things.

All "C" answers makes you a "**Victorian.**" You enjoy the finer things in life and never pass up the opportunity to smell the roses. Your clothing is soft, floral chintz, lacy and romantic. You'd rather own one perfect cameo than bangles and baubles galore. When your friends are around you they secretly envy your relaxed intuitive manner.

And finally, if you selected all "D" answers you are "**Smart n Sassy.**" You decided fresh out of kindergarten that your climb up the corporate ladder would come soon after learning how to ride a two-wheeler. Your no-nonsense approach to life carries through in all you do. Your wardrobe consists of practical, yet stylish basics—good quality blazers, beautifully tailored skirts, and a good gold chain. Your hair is simple yet elegant. Your makeup is there but never bold. Your sense of style speaks of your confidence and your ability to shun "following the crowd." But, beware of collecting a wardrobe full of strictly tailored clothes.

Did you find yourself there? What? You said there were a couple of those that sounded like you? Guess what?! You're normal. Most of us have two different fashion personalities—one for dress-up times and another for casual times. Some girls even enjoy the variety of trying out a little of each depending on where they are and what they're doing—which brings me to our next subject:

The Life You Lead and The Clothes You'll Need

Now that you know your fashion personality, can you list some of the factors that influence what you wear? Close your eyes and see how many things you can think of, then check the list below to see how well you did.

1. The dress code at school.
2. How much does it cost?
3. Does it match other garments you already have?
4. What kind of climate do you live in?
5. What do most of your friends wear?
6. Are you athletic—or ultra feminine?
7. What do you need clothes for the most? School, work, socializing?
8. The size and type of community in which you live.
9. Your coloring.
10. Your size and shape.

Did you have some of the same answers as me?

The clothing you will buy and wear will probably be in the following categories:

A. *Day time*—for school or (some day) work
Select: 1. Mix and match coordinates
2. Easy fitting knits
3. Easy care clothing
4. Wash and wear fabrics

B. *Casual wear*—after school and work, picnics and beach—any outdoor activity—or inside fun!
Select: 1. Wash and wear cottons
2. T-shirt knits
3. Look for comfort

C. *Something special*—church, special luncheon dates, art galleries and museums, etc.
Select: 1. Skirts and soft blouses
2. Nice dresses

3. Dressy pants with pretty sweaters, perhaps a little glitzy

D. *Queen for a Day*—recitals, pageants, weddings, banquets,special parties or dates
Select: 1. Old fashioned, Victorian look
2. Something swirling and feminine
3. Whatever makes you feel "extra" special
4. Soft fabrics such as velvet, organza or lace or the wonderful feel of taffeta.

Some Helpful Advice on Fabrics

Manmade (synthetic) fabrics certainly have become part of our lives. It's hard to imagine what it was like without rayon, nylon, dacron and orlon—to name a few "ons"! However, I'm sure you've noticed that natural fabrics are once again "the thing," and people everywhere are rediscovering just how comfortable, absorbent and warm natural fabrics really are.

The *synthetic* fibers:
Acetate—This shiny fiber is made from wood pulp and is usually made into fabrics that are not very expensive. It's used a lot in scarves and blouses. It wrinkles easily.
Dacron—A very strong yarn that is used with cotton and wool to help it hold its shape.
Nylon—Made from coal, air and water! The fiber is soft to the touch but very tough. Nylon is used to make stockings and hosiery, underwear, blouses and sleepwear to name a few.
Orlon—Found in sweaters and coats, it creates bulk and keeps you warm.

The *natural* fibers:
Cotton—Very durable and absorbent, dyes well, provides warmth without weight when layered, not harmed by heat. Aids in moisture evaporation to keep skin cool in summer.

Linen—Used in spring and summer, has a look of crispness (but tends to wrinkle); otherwise easy care.

Ramie—Comes from a plant with "woody" leaves grown mainly in China. It has a linen look.

Silk—Woven from the threads produced by the silkworm. Lustrous finish, should not be put in water as it will go limp. Please have dry-cleaned. Can be dyed into beautiful colors. Washable silks are available too. They look more casual and feel terrific.

Wool—Long lasting, strong fiber, spun into wool from sheep's "hair." It is absorbent, resilient (sort of stretchy, but can get pulled out of shape, too). There are a few more animal fibers besides sheep's wool that you may wear: cashmere, alpaca, mohair and camel hair.

For easy care wash and wear items such as polyester blends can be useful. Polyester by itself can be very hot and may not be a good choice in summer. Inexpensive polyester can take on a shiny, almost "plastic" look that is not very appealing and can make you look "dated."

The "naturals" allow your skin to breathe, which is much healthier anyway. The key to warmth is in the layering as much as the fabric worn.

Before we get into more of *what to wear*, let's talk about how to *take care* of what we have:

* When you buy a new garment, be certain to keep any tags attached that include laundering instructions that may not be on the sewn in tags.

* Learn the proper way to help with the laundry; separate colors, don't overload the washer, use correct water temperature, only use bleach sparingly. Use fabric softeners to cut down on wrinkles and minimize static electricity. Never over dry your clothes.

* Hang garments up to dry on **plastic** hangers only when still slightly damp; you may not need to iron. (Hurray!) If ironing is needed, get permission or have mother do it for you.

* If a garment is soiled or damaged, get it taken care of

before you forget. Never put something away that requires attention.

* Never fold or put something away that is too damp as it will mildew and acquire a musty odor.

* Don't put shoes in your closet until they have "aired out" for eight hours, and never, if they have mud or dirt on them. Shoes require weekly cleaning anyway.

* Keep jewelry separated in a dresser drawer or jewelry box to avoid tangles.

* Launder fine washables such as lingerie, lace edged hankies, stockings and underwear in a sink by hand or in one of those fabulous net washing sacks in your washing machine on gentle setting. Do not put in clothes dryer.

* Please do not establish a daily floor pile of clothing that you've taken off. Have your own pretty hamper to match your bedroom or bath.

Avoiding the Fashion Police!

Don't buy that awesome plaid coat! It looks great, but it's not for each and every occasion.

Do buy a simple, solid style that can be worn everywhere and looks great over everything. Then, by saving money, perhaps you can add the "fun" coat later.

Don't wear gargantuan, garish accessories if you are petite.

Do wear everything in proportion to your body size.

Don't allow undergarments to peek out.

Do wear slips one inch shorter than skirts and dresses, and be certain that no straps of any kind are visible under tank tops or blouses.

Don't wear what everyone else is wearing if it doesn't look right on *you*.

Do be an individual and wear only what fits properly.

Don't be a slave to fashion trends by wearing something you feel silly in just to be included or look "cool."

Do establish your own fashion statement by experimenting when you shop. Try on lots of different styles until you find the ones that are "you."

Don't wear horizontal (across) stripes on parts of your figure that may be too wide. They will work like an optical illusion and make you look huge!

Don't wear bulky turtleneck sweaters if you have a short neck or a chubby chin.

Do wear simple lines, solid colors and gentle draping of fabric to hide figure flaws.

Don't buy something that doesn't fit properly, no matter **how** much you love it.

Do hold out for perfection and don't let that money burn a hole in your pocket. (You would **never** do that, now would you?!)

Don't be a "prima-donna" when an adult takes you clothes shopping. The key word is "compromise." Moms, please note: if she hates it, she won't wear it anyway and that's a waste of hard earned dollars.

If you have a problem, *Do* be willing to try on selections that you think you may not like—you might be pleasantly surprised. One of my favorite dresses looked awful on the hanger.Smart girls simply shouldn't pout or make a scene in a store (or anywhere).

Don't "paw" through the merchandise on the racks when shopping, and refrain from showing up with the entire gang from school. Sales people don't like it when everyone crowds into the fitting room at once.

Do explain to the sales person that your mother will be there soon and that you would like to browse around while you are waiting. You are a customer and should not be treated rudely just because you are young. If you get a sales person who is unpleasant or impatient with you, leave and come back with an adult. It would serve no real purpose to argue with the person yourself. Just remember to be polite and pleasant—never silly, giggly or rude. Two wrongs never make a right, you know!

Don't leave clothing laying on the fitting room floor. Always put it back on the very same hanger—buttons buttoned, zippers zipped, and all fasteners fastened!

Do bring merchandise out of fitting room in perfect condition.

Don't buy clothing without trying it on first. You are still growing by leaps and bounds, and what fit properly last month may be way too short by now. You never know, and it sure is better to be a smart shopper than to deal with the hassles of returning merchandise.

Do look at yourself in the mirror at all angles before being satisfied enough to own something,. Lean over, reach up and bend sideways to make sure the garment is comfortable, not too tight or too short.

Take Your Cue from Color

The last time I wore a pale grey blouse and had three people ask if I had been ill was the day I decided not to wear pale grey again. (at least not near my face!)

Color has an interesting effect on how we feel about ourselves—both physically and emotionally. Bright colors can cheer us up, drab colors can make us feel less energetic. What's your favorite color? More than likely you chose a color that also looks good on your body. Did you know that it's also a good idea to do your home decorating in your best fashion colors? Have fun planning your **total** beauty look from nature's beautiful palettes.

The color of a garment often expresses the personality of the wearer.

IF YOU LIKE RED: Red is the color of vitality and action, it attracts attention and helps draw a person out. If you love red, you love life! Everyone who wears red is noticed. It puts you at the top of the rainbow. It can be bold, brash, attention getting or soft, warm and comforting...like a flickering fire on a winter's eve. Red is the splendor of royalty, the romance of a rose.

IF YOU LIKE YELLOW: Yellow is favored by the intellectual who is less emotional than red or blue. It implies a beautifully controlled temper. If it is your color, you will belittle flattery, while you long for admiration. You are unusual because you can keep a secret. Your happiest choice for a companion will be one who likes your own color or purple.

IF YOU CHOSE PINK: You have great feminine charm and people find this charm irresistible. You have excellent taste in friends and clothes. You have a gracious social manner. IF YOU CHOSE ORANGE: You possess unlimited energy. You tend to have several projects going simultaneously. Be cautious not to over-extend yourself. You are modern, inquisitive and don't mind trying new things.

IF YOU CHOSE TRUE BLUE: You are cool, dignified, sophisticated and serene. Homes decorated in blue turn into a peaceful oasis. Whether you choose the light breeze of aqua or the bold, commanding shade of navy; blue is a classic- and so are you.

IF GREEN IS YOUR CHOICE: Freshness, nature, life, luck..., green is all of these and more. It's as restful as a day in the country, lush as jungle foliage, new as the first morning of spring. Your tendency towards the natural beauty of life is as refreshing as the color itself.

IF YOU CHOSE PURPLE: You are regal, majestic and opulent. Purple inspires wealth and achieving ones goals. On the "down to earth" side of purple; cherish the violets and lilacs that this beautiful color brings to mind.

Let's not forget our neutrals and basics.

BROWN: A harvest of browns, beiges, rusts and tans bring country and city looks together. You are warm hearty, natural and self confident.

BLACK: The color of the night. You are full of mystery, drama, intrigue and power. Black is strictly for the adventurous and daring. Black worn with the right accessories—one perfect strand of pearls or a bold, bright scarf can be pure magic.

GRAY: The newest neutral in town. You are soft and

classy. Gray can be smokey, soft, sleek, sophisticated and simple—all at once!

WHITE: You're classic. Whether contemporary or country crisp—white has so many variations. The lightness of summer clouds, the softness of newly fallen snow or the delicacy of lace. White is always the right choice.

Although its fun to look up our favorite colors in "horoscope" fashion, how do you really know which ones to buy and which ones to shun? I do not advocate having colors "done" and having yourself classified as a "season" or "type" unless you haven't a clue as to what colors to wear. You don't need those limitations and restrictions placed on your imagination.

One of my favorite color combinations to wear uses two of the colors that a color consultant told me I shouldn't wear.

Take different color scarfs or remnants of fabric and drape them around your shoulders. Look at yourself in true light not fluorescent (tubular) lighting—but natural light without make- up. Well—what do you see? It will be fairly obvious to you which colors are "naturals" for you and which ones would need some real coaxing to work. Your best choices will immediately bring a glow to your skin and your eyes will sparkle. The colors that are not quite as suitable will just "sit there" doing nothing. If one of these lazy colors needs to be worn (perhaps a bridesmaid dress or a uniform—you know, no choice) then get out the cosmetic box. Start experimenting with complementary eye shadow shades, blushes and lip colors.

This is where a color wheel will come in handy. An art supply store or a decorating center will have a color wheel. You can experiment with color combinations that otherwise you might never try—avocado with grape, goldenrod with cornflower blue—the possibilities are really fun. For example, colors that are directly opposite one another on the color wheel are complimentary. Indian brown (a shade of orange) and federal blue slate are opposites on the wheel, and although you may not readily put these two colors together, you may be surprised at the way they seem to work.

Wearing Color as a Cosmetic

Colors worn on your body—especially near you face, can have a very complimentary effect on you hair, eyes and teeth. However, the wrong colors can really create a disastrous illusion.

For example:

- If you have blood-shot eyes, wearing pink or red can exaggerate the condition.

- If your tooth enamel is dingy or yellowish, wearing gold or yellow near your face will make your teeth look dreadful!

- If you color your hair and for some reason it has ended up in a brassy shade of blonde or red, wearing brassy shades of yellow, red gold or silver near your face will set your hair on "fire"!

The Basics Stay the Same

The basics of fashion really do stay the same. If they didn't it would be impossible to have this chapter on fashion. We all stay up to date by following trends and fads to some extent. But, the basic rules of fashion are the mainstay that help us to really plan a good wardrobe.

A girl with a strong sense of fashion coupled with a secure sense of who she is can really have some fun stretching and bending some of the fashion rules to make them work for her. I'm going to list the basic rules in this section in reference form so that you may look up what you need to know when you need it.

Let's remember to have confidence when we shop, use our imagination but don't ignore the basic rules that **never** change.

Here's a few:

-The four main factors that influence what we wear are: age, figure, current fashion and where you're going.

- Basic colors and neutrals: black, brown, navy, beige, white, grey (wise to use for major purchases such as coats, boots, good wool skirts, etc.)

- Buy clothes that have versatility and can be worn during more than one season.

- Buy as little as possible that *must* be dry cleaned.

- Don't purchase by impulse—think about what you buy carefully.

- Take a fashion inventory to clear out the mistakes, out- of-dates, etc.

- Do your purchases reflect the true image that you wish to portray?

- Start your "good" jewelry purchases with gold and silver so that you'll always have something to match. Add the "fun" pieces gradually.

- Don't dress with more than four horizontal cuts at one time. For example, neckline, waistline, hemline, strap across ankle on shoes. More than four different colors, such as adding different layers in different colors can make you look short and "dumpy."

- Wear the proper make-up for the clothing you're wearing. Remember too, that **without** make-up, you can't wear something that with make-up would look better. Example black, white or beige garments can really wash you out with no make-up.

- Every outfit should have a *focal point*. A focal point or main point of interest should be near your face if possible.

A Glossary of Fashion Terms

Classic – A style or design that starts out by satisfying a basic need and then endures as being acceptable by a large number of people for an extended period of time. Examples of **classics** would be a pump, loafer, cardigan sweater or an A-line skirt. Variations will occur, but the basic design remains the same.

Fad – A short-lived fashion trend. Fads are here today

145

and gone tomorrow. They are often influenced by the entertainment industry. Think about how many times you may have considered copying a "look" make popular by your favorite singer or actress.

Fashion – Styles which are accepted by a large group at any given time.

High Fashion – Styles which are accepted by a more limited, perhaps more elite or fashion conscious group of people. High Fashion is often influenced by the rich, the famous and the "royal."

Fashion and Figures

Clothes affect the way we look and feel psychologically as well as the way we feel physically. Look below to understand your figure type then choose clothing that will compliment or camouflage your shape.

Wide Middles and Tummy Bulges — Wear loose, easy unfitted styles. Avoid body hugging or straight line silhouettes.

Heavy Legs — Pants and skirts worn below the knee are great disguises. Deep toned hose give a slimmer look. Avoid skirts and pants that are too narrow.

Wide Hips and Heavy Thighs — Most skirt styles are fine, except the very straight and narrow. Tunics and big tops are great for camouflage. Avoid pleated pants and tops that end at the hipline.

Short Legs — Straight leg pants and skirts worn below the knee give height. Jumpsuits and dresses offer a vertical effect. Tops and bottoms that match create a longer look, too. High heels add inches.

Too Thin — Full skirts give an illusion of added depth. Wide pants make legs appear fuller. Clothing that is too bare or body hugging makes figure appear thinner.

Too Heavy — Styles should be simple and have linear appearance. Jackets and sweaters should cover hips. Any vertical line or continuation of color is slimming.

And, last but not least, these helpful hints for *all* figure types will help you to plan the perfect wardrobe:

- Curved lines emphasize roundness
- Straight lines are slimming
- Bulky fabrics add weight and width
- Clingy fabrics highlight any problem
- Prints, stripes and plaids should be in proportion to your body frame.

Lots of teens have figure flaws—perfect bodies are few and far between. Accent the positive and play down the negative. You'll change your fashion image and personality many times. Wearing what's right for you—not just what's in or what may be right for everyone else, will add a perfect "Finishing Touch" to your puzzle.

IV.

So You Want to be a Model . . .

Chapter 12
Modeling—Is it For You?

There it is. That WORD. It drew you to this chapter like a magnet! I can think of no other subject more likely to conjure up visions of grandeur in teenage girls than modeling.

I was certainly no different than you are. I guess the "bug" really hit me when I was eleven or twelve. I would sit mesmerized for hours over fashion magazines and profiles on famous models—especially Wilhelmina.

My friend's brother had a camera and wanted some of my friends and I to sit for pictures. Harmless enough, right? Well, maybe—maybe not! You should never let anyone take your picture without your parents' approval.

As it was, my family knew the aspiring photographer and my father took me to the house and stayed while the photographs were being taken. Gee! Funny how I thought those pictures were *so* good back then, and how hideous I would think they looked now. (Yes, I destroyed them long ago!) But, I learned a lot from that first photo session. I discovered how much weight the camera can "add" to your image—up to ten pounds! I also saw how awkward your legs can look if you are not standing properly. Pictures really *don't* lie!

Nonetheless, I was determined to pursue my dream! I wanted so desperately to attend one of the local modeling schools. But it cost hundreds of dollars and my parents were somewhat hesitant. During this same time I became involved in a wonderful program offered in my school—Junior Achievement.

Junior Achievement, or JA as it's called, combines business professionals in the community with students who have set their sights to a particular career, or just want to gain some hands-on business training from the "pros."

To say that it changed my life is an understatement. But how did the business world have anything to do with modeling? Well, business and modeling have *everything* to do with each other! I'll explain.

The JA "company" (like a club) I joined was sponsored

by a local radio station. Not only was I interested in modeling, but *anything* to do with entertainment or broadcasting. Our group wrote, produced, and recorded our own 30 minute radio program which aired each Sunday night. At the end of the year awards were presented and I was honored with President of the Year and Miss Junior Achievement. Well guess what the prize was for Miss JA? A full scholarship to the modeling school I had dreamed of attending!

I was on my way. From the part-time modeling jobs I was able to do on weekends I purchased my first car—a baby blue 1966 Mustang. With my driver's license and my dad not having to be a chauffeur any more I was available for more jobs and really became quite busy after graduation from high school.

Sound easy? It really wasn't. *Now* I have the truthful task of giving you the *real* scoop. I'm going to tell you the good, the bad, and everything in between about the exciting world of modeling.

Many girls turn the dream of modeling into reality. Maybe you can too. But there's more to becoming a model than just wishing for it.

Having what it takes to model in your hometown may differ a great deal from what it takes to model in New York, Los Angeles, or other larger metropolitan areas. For "hometown" work, you will almost always be required to go through a self-improvement/modeling course with the school/agency you wish to become affiliated with. More than likely, you will be asked to incur the expense of photographs for a portfolio (book of pictures) or composite (card of photographs showing your different "looks.") Between the class and the photographs you could easily spend up to $2,500.00 (even more depending on where you live).

Now, even if your parents would consider this expense—are you *really* sure you want to do it? Also, keep in mind that *NO REPUTABLE* school will promise or assure you that modeling jobs are guaranteed at the completion of your course. If the owner or sales counselor does make a promise of work, you know immediately that you're in the WRONG PLACE. Don't sign *anything*. Just go home. You see, half of the success of a model is determined by her personality, determination, and sense of responsibility. The other half certainly is based on outer attributes but—how does this person at the modeling school know enough about you from one interview to determine whether or not you are dependable and energetic (even when you don't feel like it) and impeccably groomed at all times? Well, there's no way that anyone can get a real feel for your qualities and determination unless they spend time observing you for a fairly long period.

The instructor and school/agency director will have an opportunity to see if you get frustrated easily in class when trying something new (are you apt to do the same thing if sent on an assignment to an important client?) Are you consistent? I once had a student in modeling class who, after spending hundreds of dollars on a portfolio drastically changed her hairstyle! When I asked why she had made such a radical decision, she replied, "Gee, I saw it the other day on a model in a magazine and thought it was really neat!" Not only were her pictures obsolete, but her spontaneity made the agency director a little nervous. Imagine how it would look for the agency to think they were sending the client a blonde with shoulder length straight hair for a bridal show, and have the client call to say, "Why did you send me a girl with a brown bob?" Don't laugh, it has happened.

So, have you got what it takes?

1. *Will it bother you to have someone (besides your folks!) advise you on what you should and shouldn't do with your looks and other personal habits?* It *will* happen, and it's done by professionals in the modeling business who know what "look" and image is necessary for your success. Let's face it—if you are successful, so is your agent so it just makes sense that they will advise you when necessary.

2. *Do you fit the physical requirements?* Yes, I know—your least favorite part—but it's reality my dear! These physical requirements will differ slightly based on whether the modeling you aspire to do will be the "small town" variety or leaving on the next jet for New York. Actually, they don't differ too much, so I am including the following chart as a guideline. Charts of this type are not only helpful to those of you who are interested in modeling, but also offer helpful advice for knowing what your measurements should be based on your height and weight.

Remember, how old you are chronologically does not necessarily determine your category.

Junior Teen
Height 5'7" to 5'8" (in stocking feet)
Average weight 100 to 118 pounds
Bust 32" to 34"
Waist 21" to 24"
Hips 32" to 34"
These are the girls who must have a strictly youthful "girl-next-door" look. They should look no older than sixteen or seventeen, and should wear clothing sizes 5 to 9.

Missy
Height 5'7" to 5'9" (in stocking feet)
Average weight 105 to 120 pounds
Bust 33" to 34"
Waist 20" to 23"
Hips 33" to 35"
The "in-between" look of a Missy model is somewhat older than a teen but not yet "haute couture."

High Fashion
Height 5'8" to 6' (in stocking feet)
Average weight 110 to 130 pounds
Bust 33" to 34"
Waist 23" to 25"
Hips 34" to 35"
Girls who fall into this category have what you probably will recognize as a typical model "look." High cheekbones, ultra sleek, sophisticated, but above all—a beautiful "uniqueness" all their own.

Are you wondering just *who* this person is who arbitrarily made up these stringent rules, heights, and weights that may have dashed your hopes for fame and fortune? Actually, it's done by the fashion industry for basically two reasons: First, the camera adds the appearance of an extra five to ten pounds to each person. Second, models must be able to wear manufacturers' samples with no alterations straight off the rack.

I will tell you from experience that there is little or no flexibility in those measurements found in the fashion capitals of the world. It's "stand up to the measuring tape—sorry honey—goodbye," more often than not. This can be a heart-breaking ordeal where your hopes and dreams are higher than the clouds. It doesn't really matter that you have a beautiful face, gorgeous hair, and that you've done all the Back to School shows for your local agency or department store. If you're only 5'4" you are not going to be signed by a New York agency.

3. *Are you healthy?*

On the surface, you may perceive modeling as strictly fun and glamour with a big monetary pay off. WRONG. Modeling is mostly hard work. Many models work five days a week or more with their day beginning at six in the morning. If you had stayed up too late the night before you'd look like it. Modeling is competitive, and you cannot afford mistakes. Do you eat properly and exercise regularly? Your health and stamina are vital to your success. Did you know that some models have had to stand under bright lights in high heels for hours on end? How about modeling heavy woolens outside when its 90 degrees? I've done it—and you'll count your blessings if you were already in good shape and healthy.

4. *Are you comfortable in front of the camera?*

Do you photograph well? Some girls never do, even though they are lovely in person, and some girls who are not terribly striking in person photograph like a million bucks! It takes a lot of practice but you can acquire more confidence in front of the camera by having a friend or family member take some practice or "test" shots, as well as my favorite when I was a teenager—practice "shots" in front of a full-length mirror. I could be by myself if I felt self-conscious. It also gave me an opportunity to practice certain poses or facial expressions before the camera recorded the "real thing"

5. Can you handle rejection?
No one person can possibly be right for everything. Makes sense, doesn't it? However, the first time it's you who isn't right is not easy. If you're not right for one particular assignment, please be pleasant anyway, as that client may be able to use you in the future.

"Almost" isn't good enough in the modeling business either. One little chipped nail that you can hardly notice could be the "kiss of death." You may feel as though you are being examined under a microscope when you visit a prospective client, but you must also remember that lots of money is being spent for that individual to promote his or her product.

6. Are you intelligent?
I don't mean are you seeking your Ph.D.—however, the days of "blonde, beautiful, and dumb" are long gone.

A girl who is shallow, not well read or interested in life will come across visually as a rather empty soul.

A good model is an interesting person—not just interesting looking

7. Do you manage your money well?
Nothing lasts forever, and while you may be one of the lucky few to capture a successful career, you may not be making money consistently. For example, ethnic models may be "in vogue" today and may be riding the crest of success but what happens when the trend changes one day? It will—because trends *always* change.

A smart model will have a career backup as well as a strong savings account and secure investments when necessary. While Dad doesn't need to contact his Stock Broker if you're only doing hometown modeling assignments, a young girl who finds herself in the big time will have many new concerns.

Remember, modeling—even on a "local" level can be an excellent stepping stone to other careers or related fields. I know so many girls who have landed wonderful jobs in the cosmetic field as a result of a client they once worked for. Jobs in public relations, fashion coordination and special events are also possible, to name a few.

I started out modeling in a local department store but held onto my love of writing and teaching charm and modeling classes. Look what happened!

8. *Are you a prima-donna?*
"It's too hot..."
"It's too cold..."
"I broke a nail..."
"This is taking so-o-o long!"
"I'm hungry..."
Oh **please**! Even if you're a good model, no one will want to put up with this behavior for very long.

Things don't always go right. If you're doing a photo shoot outdoors and it begins to drizzle, I'm sure the photographer will try to wait it out. I've killed time (cheerfully!) for hours while lights in a television studio were replaced, re-set, and re-adjusted. But, guess what? That same client asked for me time and time again for their commercials because I was cooperative and easy to get along with (always pack a good novel!)

Above all, remember that as much of a cliche as it may sound—you must be *more—much more—than just another pretty face.*

Chapter 13
Fashion Related Careers
and The Job Search Adventure

If you're like most teens, you enjoyed reading the section on modelling. Even if it's not your own personal passion it probably still intrigues you. But what about those of you who simply will not be able to pursue a career in modelling for any number of legitimate reasons? If you are 4'10" and no one in your family is over 5'1", you may want to set your sights on an alternative.

For example, if you have artistic talent and love fashion, then perhaps a career in fashion design or illustration is on the horizon.

In this section we'll discuss some possibilities. I have chosen to not list average starting salaries as they vary greatly from region to region.

The best advice I can give to you is to meet and talk with someone who works at the career you're interested in. Ask them questions regarding work conditions, room for advancement and growth potential in your market. (area in which you live and work) Ask if you may take notes.

The career you choose will account for how you occupy most of your waking hours. Needless to say, it needs to be an activity you'll continue to enjoy and be challenged by for many years.

ACTRESS

Qualifications
  Ability to memorize scripts
  Ability to portray characters in a convincing way
  Ability to speak clearly
  Attractive
  Creative
  Resilient

Possible Places of Employment
  Advertising Agency
  Film Company
  Drama school

Television or radio station
Theater

Training and Education
A school or college specializing in dramatic arts is desirable. Individual instruction with a drama coach can be extremely helpful.

Possible Negative Aspects
Frequent travel (also a positive)
Long hours of rehearsal
Must memorize many pages of script
Possibility of rejection on a regular basis
Probability of working a second job while becoming established

ART DIRECTOR

Qualifications
Artistic
Creative
Ability to visualize
Work well under pressure
Ability to adhere to deadlines
Be perceptive and understanding of other people's needs
Must stay up to date on market trends

Possible Employment
In-house (on premises) advertising departments of business and industries
Advertising Agencies
Graphic Arts Studios
Department Stores
Self-employment

Training and Education
Bachelor's degree with major in art or at least three years of training at an accredited art school

Possible Negative Aspects
Must take the chance of rejection after spending long hours working on a project.

May spend many years after school work is complete in lesser jobs.

DANCER

Qualifications
Excellent Health
Excellent Physical Condition
Graceful
Self-Disciplined
Strong sense of determination
Superb Stamina

Possible Employment
Dance School Instructor - many instructors eventually own their own studio
Theater Company
Professional Dance Company
Cruise Ships
Theme Parks (often seasonal)

Training and Education
Courses in drama and music theory helpful
Extensive dance training; first in a classroom, then privately
Bachelor's degree is not essential, but helpful if you are serious about the career

Possible Negative Aspects
Long hours of strenuous training
Possible insecurity, initially
Starting pay can be quite low
Probability of working a second job at first
Possible rejection following many auditions

FLIGHT ATTENDANT

Qualifications
  Healthy
  Able to handle emergency situations
  Ability to communicate tactfully and effectively
  Organized
  Poised
  Pleasing Personality
  Height and Weight restrictions (airlines vary)
  Willingness to travel
  Willingness to relocate

Possible Employment
  Commercial Airlines
  Military Services

Training and Education
  College degree required for some airlines
  Each airline provides an extensive training program
for newly hired flight attendants as well as regular
refresher courses.

Possible Negative Aspects
  Must adhere to rigid schedule
  Must adapt to critical situations
  Must remain calm under pressure

FASHION DESIGNER

Qualifications
  Artistic
  Creative
  Imaginative
  Knowledge of Fashion Trends
  Knowledge of Fashion Basics
  Knowledge of Marketing Fundamentals

Possible Employment

Clothing Manufacturers
Self Employment
Fashion designers who employ assistants

Training and Education
After college, at least three years of training in art and fashion at an accredited design school. An apprenticeship with a reputable firm both during and after schooling is not only beneficial, but most likely, necessary to break into such a competitive field.

Possible Negative Aspects
May work at lower pay for many years as an assistant before "breaking into" the fashion business.

INTERIOR DESIGNER

Qualifications
Artistic
Organized
Creative
Excellent eye for color, texture and design basics
Business minded
Ability to understand client's personal needs

Possible Employment
Department Stores
Architecture or design firms
Furniture or Fabric Companies
Self-employment

Training and Education
Bachelor's degree in interior design
Degree from an accredited art school with emphasis on interior design
Apprenticeship with a reputable interior design firm is desirable

Possible Negative Aspects
Some firms pay on "commission only" basis
May end up working as a salesperson in a furniture store

Possibility of working at low salary during apprenticeship

OTHER RESOURCES

These are just a few ideas. You'll think of others and you'll eventually need more specifics on each one. The following resources may be very helpful:

- Brochures and books from your local library
- Career resource publications
- Informal interviews with individuals working in the field
- School counselors
- School-sponsored "career days"

Tell me if this sounds familiar - "Why do I have to learn algebra? I'm not going to be a mathematician or a scientist. It doesn't have *anything* to do with what *I* want to be."
The skills that you acquire in school can lay the foundation that will be necessary for the pursuit of your career goals. Remember, good study habits and self-discipline will prepare you for many challenges ahead.

In choosing any career, first consider these factors:

- Your special talents
- Your hobbies
- Salary requirement
- Your lifestyle
- Education limitations, if any
- desirable work atmosphere

Some girls know right from the beginning what career path they'll follow. Others have varied interests making the choice more difficult. Perhaps you can find a perfect "marriage" of several interests and mesh them into one wonderful career objective tailor-made for you.
That's what I did. I was able to blend my love of

writing, teaching, acting, modelling and the joy of helping young girls and teens realize their full potential into the perfect career. You can too. Really!

There's a lot of difference between a job and a career.

A Job
- Can be boring
- Can be menial
- Can be something you simply *have* to do
- Is often task oriented
- Can make you feel trapped

A Career
- Allows you to utilize your interests and talents
- Allows you to grow and change
- Allows you to be in charge of your future
- Becomes a welcomed part of your life

How to Apply for a job

Your first job may be babysitting or helping around the house with special projects for compensation. These first jobs are a little easier because they are done for people you already know. But what about that first *real* job? I guarantee that the prospective employer will notice you and be impressed with your enthusiasm and professionalism if you follow these guidelines.

- Have a resume or a short personal biography. If this is your first job and you have no prior employment experience you'll want to highlight school activities, clubs and civic organizations, church involvement and volunteer work. Your resume should also indicate whether you are a permanent resident of the community, have a drivers license, have excellent health and enjoy particular hobbies and sports. This resume should be typed black on white or ecru paper. You should have an adult look it over before you distribute it.

- Lots of teens find jobs through friends or family

members's existing jobs. Lauren's dad may need a messenger to help deliver mail in his office building after school. Katie's mom could use some of your fashion expertise this summer at her clothing shop.

- If you are starting from scratch check newspapers, community bulletin boards, church bulletins and your school counselor. Your state or local employment commission may also provide some ideas.

- If the advertisement says to phone for an appointment do not show up "cold." If it reads "apply in person", please don't call. If you must call, write down everything you want to say on a sheet of paper first and practice saying it until you are relaxed. Don't be wordy. Be short, smart, to the point and speak *clearly*. If the person sounds too busy to talk, you should ask if there is a convenient time for you to come in.

- To apply in person or for an interview, wear a dress or nice skirt and blouse. What if the job itself will require that you wear shorts, slacks or even jeans? Wear a dress or skirt anyway - it will show professionalism, maturity and pride in your appearance. Keep hair and make up simple and neat. And remember please do not chew gum! Remember that you only have one chance to make a good first impression.

- Be five minutes early for your appointment. Not *too* early, never right "on the dot", and never late. If you suspect you will be late place a phone call to the individual immediately explaining your dilemma.

- Sell your strong points to counteract the possibility and probability that you lack experience. If the prospective employer still hesitates but you sense that he or she likes you, offer to work for a day or two on a trial with no pay. The employer will be impressed with your diligence and enthusiasm. Chances are the job will become permanent - with permanent spending money!

- Follow up with a short hand-written thank you note immediately after your interview. This should be addressed directly to the person who interviewed you. Mention that you appreciated the time spent for the interview and that you look forward to the possibility of working with their organization. If you feel that it is appropriate and that it wouldn't be too pushy, a phone call can be placed to the interviewer the following day. In sight - in mind!

- Even if you felt the interview didn't go well a thank-you note is a nice touch. You never know!

- Don't bring friends or family members with you for a job interview or even a "go-see."

- Last but not least; after you've landed this wonderful job don't forget these pointers:
    - always be on time
    - dress appropriately
    - no excessive talking or goofing off on the job
    - obey all rules
    - always be grateful for your job
    - Remember the positive first impression you make during your interview. Continue that positive attitude each and every day.

While you're young the sky's the limit. You can be anything you **want** to be if you want it badly enough. It will likely take sacrifice, discipline and hard work. But, the future rewards will surely be worthwhile. I call this "want" being "hungry" for it! If your goal exists in your dreams, it can turn into a reality. Believe in yourself and your capabilities.

Successfully putting together your own personal "puzzle" of self-confidence, self-esteem, inner and outer beauty and achieving a level of intelligence that you can be proud of will contribute to a beautiful future.

The End is Just the Beginning

Being a girl never included more advantages than it does today. So many doors are open for you if you'll just take the time to pursue the possibilities.

I hope this book will open doors of discovery for you. But, what I hope for most is that the doors will continue to open for many, many years with the same excitement and enthusiasm as they do now.

Find your strengths, your loves, and your talents. Work on becoming secure and comfortable with these things. Set lifetime goals based on those factors and you will always be true to yourself.

I'd like to share something with you that I cut out of a newspaper many years ago:

Teen Creed

Don't let your parents down,
They brought you up.
Be humble enough to obey.
You may be giving the orders someday.
Choose companions with care,
You become what they are.
Guard your thoughts
What you think, you become.
Choose only a date
Who would make a good mate. (But don't rush it!)
Be master of your habits,
Or they will master you.
Don't be a show off when you drive.
Drive with safety and arrive alive.
Don't let the crowd pressure you,
Stand for something, or you'll fall for anything.
                              Author Unknown

Thank you for reading this book. I hope it's been the perfect "Finishing Touch" for you!

If you'd like information on *Pretty Me Seminars* for girls

170

ages 6 to 11, or *Finishing Touches for Teens Seminars* for girls
ages 12 to 17 in your area, write to:
Finishing Touches
A Division of Pretty Me, Inc.
1240 Warner Hall Drive
Virginia Beach, Virginia 23454
or phone (804) 427-3814
(Retail and wholesale inquiries are welcome.)